# Use Your "Useless" Degree!

How to Use Your Humanities Degree in a Career as a Freelance Editor and Writer

by Kathrin Herr, The Writing Mechanic

*The Writing Mechanic Publishing Collective, Kathrin Herr*
Website: www.KathrinHerr.com
Contact email address (for permissions questions and other inquiries): thewritingmechanic@gmail.com.

Formatted and Designed by Kathrin Herr, The Writing Mechanic, KathrinHerr.com

Copyright © 2018 Kathrin Herr, The Writing Mechanic Publishing Collective.

Published by *The Writing Mechanic Publishing Collective.*

The publisher does not control or assume responsibility for author or third-party websites or their content.

USE YOUR "USELESS" DEGREE

All rights reserved.
No part of this book may be reproduced, scanned, or distributed in any printed or electronic form without permission of Kathrin Herr, The Writing Mechanic.

ISBN: 978-0-9989760-2-0

Printed in the USA by Kindle Direct Publishing print-on-demand.
Also available in e-book format through Amazon Kindle Direct Publishing.

This book is dedicated to my teachers and mentors. You gave me a chance to show and grow my talents and encouraged me to pursue my dreams:

Michael Martin
Jan Everhart
David Wolf
John Pauley

I also dedicate this book to some of my awesome clients:

Ned Pelger
Steve & Mary Lowe
Michael Munger

## Table of Contents

| | |
|---|---:|
| Introduction | 7 |
| How I Make Money Using My "Useless" Degree | 11 |

### PART 1: EDITING SKILLS & KNOWHOW — 19

| | |
|---|---:|
| Types of Editing | 21 |
| What You Need to Know | 31 |
| Word? Word. | 37 |
| Style Guides | 65 |
| Self-Publishing | 71 |
| eBooks | 81 |
| Cover Design on Canva.com | 87 |

### PART 2: BUSINESS-EY THINGS — 93

| | |
|---|---:|
| Business Formation & Money Talk | 95 |
| Get Online | 103 |
| Social Media | 111 |
| Growing Your Network | 121 |
| Pricing & Finding Work | 127 |
| Editing Tests | 139 |

### PART 3: GETTING INTO THE GROOVE — 143

| | |
|---|---:|
| Editor's Letters | 145 |
| Client Correspondence | 151 |
| Scaling Your Editing Business & Diversifying Your Income | 159 |
| The Writing Editor | 165 |
| A Day in the Editing Life | 171 |

### APPENDICES — 183

**APPENDIX A. RESOURCES FOR FREELANCERS**     **184**
**APPENDIX B. NICHE ZONE WORKSHEET**     **186**
**APPENDIX C. FREELANCER'S DAY PLANNING WORKSHEETS**     **188**

## ABOUT THE AUTHOR     193

## ACKNOWLEDGEMENTS     195

# Introduction

This book is for the wannabe free spirits who also recognize the necessity of making money. I hope that is *all* of you.

This book is for the planners who fight an internal battle between wanting to have consistent income and wanting to be passionate about their work.

This book is for the students of history, English, literature, religion, women and gender studies, philosophy, and the "soft" sciences who have heard the question, "What are you going to do with your degree?" too many times to count.

**I wrote this book for all of the humanities students—like me—who don't or didn't have a clear life path in mind following graduation.**

I know you recognize the value of your degree, as I do, but recognizing that value and learning how to translate it into a career with unlimited earning potential are two very different tasks.

Thankfully, those two tasks require the same mindset:

**In order to be successful as a humanities graduate, you must recognize the value of your degree, keep the passion for the subject matter, and pursue that passion in a tangible career field.**

This book will give you all the tools you need to become a freelance editor and writer for books and projects in our favorite genres of history, philosophy, religion, English, literature, women and gender studies, psychology, art, and creative writing—and actually make *money* at it.

If you're reading this book, I assume you already have a base knowledge of grammar, punctuation, word choice, and syntax or that you have some form of writing "gift." I will not be teaching you those basics in this book...and I am not even going to *attempt* to give you a passion for writing. That is something you need to have already learned or discovered in your humanities degree.

What I offer in this book is everything I had to learn following graduation in order to become a successful freelance editor and writer.

I'm Kathrin, and I'm a proud humanities grad.

I've always known what *kind* of work I wanted to do...

I love words. I've always loved words. But I wasn't a lover of words in the "I read a book a day" kind of way.

I was a lover of the *crafting* of words. Whether writing my own stories, performing spoken word poetry, or moving words and phrases around in a sentence to make it sound "pretty," the *crafting* of words has always been my thing.

When faced with immanent graduation in 2013 and the terrifying idea of being a "real adult," I had to make a choice: follow a set route and do work I don't love or make my own path and find a way to do the work I love...and, you know, make money to live off of.

I think I made the right choice.

And now I'm going to help you make that same choice and totally ROCK it.

Success takes work. This career is no different.

But as one of my professors once told me, "When you find the kind of work you can get lost in, that's the moment you know what you're meant to do."

So use this book to learn the skills you need to have in order to be able to do the kind of work with words that you can "get lost in."

Let's get lost together (and make some serious money at it).

# 1

## How I Make Money Using My "Useless" Degree

When I first got to college in 2009, I thought I wanted to be a communications major. Then I thought I would major in music. Then I decided to design my own major in multimedia writing. But by the end of my second year, I had settled on a major in religion.

It was a subject I was interested in, it required the most writing of any major at my school, and my professors were supportive of my talents and goals. I could give you a whole litany on the value of a liberal arts education for the growth of the publishing market, but suffice it to say I recognized early on that my degree would lead me to a rewarding, fulfilling, and life-long career few people my age are willing or able to pursue.

I graduated in 2013 from a private, liberal arts college in Iowa (Simpson College, represent!) with my BA in religion.

I can't tell you how many times I heard, "What are you going to do with *that*?" when I told people in the real world what I had majored in.

The world tends to think solely in terms of production. If you can't *produce* a useable, marketable, scalable product, you're useless. If you can't get rich quick with your productions, or at least earn a $70k salary right out of college, you're not doing it right—whatever "it" is.

Humanities majors hear the same questions repeatedly:

> *What are you going to do after graduation?*
>
> *What **useful** skills are you learning in your classes?*
>
> *How are you going to use your degree to make a difference in the world?*

To me, the hilarious part about those questions is that few people outside of the humanities think the abstract skills we learn in religion, history, English, women and gender studies, and philosophy will be useful in our quest to produce meaningful and scalable products.

When they ask us what we are going to do with our humanities degrees, what they are really asking is:

## ***How are you going to make money?!***

### The Perks of Our "Useless" Degrees

In our "useless" degrees, we learned how to ask the big questions.

We learned how to research, think, write, and communicate. We learned how to create, change, and inspire the world around us. We learned the power of the written word to *heal and protect* people. We learned the power of the written word to *connect* people.

I chose to major in religion, but my choice did not mean I intended to go into the ministry. I chose religion for the volume of writing it required, the one-on-one relationships with my professors it facilitated, and the fact that I always had more questions than answers (and that I wasn't the only one questioning).

I learned how to edit words because I had to write and edit, A LOT. I learned how to ask questions that most often led to more questions. I learned to be content in my state of inconclusiveness and lack of discernment. I learned how to talk to people intelligently, love people well, and disagree with people...usually lovingly.

And though it wasn't my intent, my religion major opened up a vast world of clientele for my editing business. Because I speak the theology language, I have been able to work for pastors who wrote books for their congregations and authors of spiritual memoir. My degree gave me my editing niche and allowed me to create a job I love. I even got to throw in other parts of my personality into the mix, editing humorous books like *Great Sex, Christian Style* by Ned Pelger—one of my favorite books by one of my favorite friends I've never actually met face-to-face.

Furthermore, my education cultivated in me an affinity for life-long learning. In my classes, I was consistently challenged to read new types of literature, engage in new kinds of media, learn new technology and skills, and communicate with people from all different backgrounds and opinions.

I learned *how to learn* by adapting to different situations in my educational formation. Nowadays, I often have to figure out website design, DNS settings (...wait, what are they again?), cover design software, video editing software, a new social media platform, or genre-specific language I'm not familiar with. I am able to *learn* to handle each new situation or issue that comes up because I *learned how to learn* in my religion degree.

I'm a **life-long learner**.

I'm a runner, and I love the meme about track and cross-country that says, "My sport is your sport's punishment." In humanities degrees, our most cultivated skill—our "sport"—is the skill most other degree programs despise and are "punished" with.

That skill is...wait for it... **WRITING**. (dun, dun, dun...)

We write argumentative papers with persuasive arguments. We write research papers with three pages of citations and 50+ footnotes. We write personal essays. We write fiction and poetry. We write descriptive or evaluative papers on works of literature. We write discussions of literary troupes and mechanisms and conventions. We even write journal entries.

And we are often asked to engage in peer revision. We trade papers with a fellow student, read, give notes, and provide constructive feedback. We "edit" each other's work.

And then our professors (most of whom are stellar writers themselves) grade and provide feedback on our papers and return them to us so we can review the feedback and use it to do better (or *even* better) on the next paper.

The structure of our class assignments have prepped us for greatness as editors and writers...and we didn't even have to suffer (too much).

My humanities degree also taught me to be an autonomous thinker and to accomplish goals by deadlines I set for myself.

In my senior year, I had to complete a large thesis paper project that included creative writing, research, and biblical interpretation. I had due dates to meet throughout the semester, but I was for the most part left to my own production schedule. I had to be self-motivated in order to get the research done, the 1700-word poem written, complete the extensive biblical interpretation, and prepare my final presentation. I didn't have anyone holding my hand making sure I got my work done.

Being self-motivated to complete projects like this primed me for freelance work. I still have deadlines to meet, but I work from home, and I have to set work schedules for myself that will allow me to meet those deadlines. I have to decide when to start and finish my work day...and when or when to not put on pants. No one holds my hand as I copyedit a 400-page book in two weeks. No one writes out a work schedule for me when I have a publishing project that will take one month to complete and requires 100 different tasks and details to remember and execute.

The structure of my humanities degree gave me the autonomy to succeed as a freelancer.

## Why Freelance?

The term "freelance" has a somewhat negative connotation. Freelance work has often been equated with doing valuable work for next to nothing for payment.

I'm surprised at how many people think freelancers are the "market rejects"—the editors who weren't good enough to get jobs at big publishing companies or news organizations.

But here is the truth—a truth I've learned in my nearly eight years working in the publishing world as a freelance editor: Publishing companies today are laying off their full-time editors and throwing them into their own freelance pools.

With the burgeoning popularity of self-publishing and the rapid growth of the eBook empire, traditional publishing is slowly becoming a thing of the past—part of a "good-ole-days" portrait—and many traditional publishers can't afford to keep full-time copyeditors on salary.

While the majority of university presses still seem to be going strong, the job pool for those salaried positions are limited to a short list of editors with 20+ years of experience in an "inner circle," so even the best editor right out of undergrad is unqualified for such a position. And even university presses use freelancers more often than they hire salaried editors (but you still need 20+ years of experience working for a major publishing house or press...so you should have started when you were two years old).

What's more, major companies like Meredith Corp. who still keep a number of editors on staff tend to promote in-house: their interns become their assistants become their editors become their executives. And even in those companies, long-time salaried editors have been laid off and added to a list of freelancers.

So how can you, a 20-something fresh from your humanities degree, break into the publishing world?

Start your own freelance editing services company.

### Should You Be a Freelance Editor?

Entrepreneurship does not make for an easy life, friends. Before you gear up to take the self-employment plunge, do a gut-and-character check:

- Are you a go-getter?
- Are you willing to learn necessary skills—and never stop learning?
- Are you willing to sacrifice parts of other things—a social life, for example—for the sake of doing the preliminary work to build your business?
- Are you willing to ask for help (monetary help included)?
- Are you a collaborative learner?
- Are you good at grammar?
- Are you a good writer?
- Are you willing to do professional development exercises to improve your talents and skills?

- Are you detail oriented?
- Are you going to put in the time and effort necessary to build your business?

If you answered yes to those questions, you just might have what it takes to be a successful freelance editor!

In this book, I am going to give you all the other tools you need to successfully launch your freelance editing business. It's a long process and it takes a ton of work.

I won't lie and tell you it will be easy. But it will most definitely be worth it.

And by the time you finish this book, you will be able to answer the question, "How are you, a humanities major, going to make money?" with a simple statement:

"I'm going to make money as a professional freelance writer and editor."

# Part 1: Editing Skills & Knowhow

# 2

## Types of Editing

First thing's first: What is editorial freelancing?

Though I hope you know at least part of the answer to that question already—since you bought this book—there are different types of editing you can do as a freelancer, and discovering the type you're best at and like doing the most can help you hone in on your editing niche and build your business with ideal clients.

I'll go into detail about each type of editing, but first, answer the following questions to determine which type of editing you are particularly inclined toward:

When I read a book, I mostly notice...
    a. the plotline and character development.
    b. the writer's style.
    c. errors in grammar and punctuation.
    d. how well the author adhered to common style rules, such as the Oxford comma and correct use of "that" and "which."

My first inclination when I have a text to edit is to...
    a. read through the whole text and make comments.
    b. get a sense of the writer's voice.

    c.   pull out my red pen and start slashing away.
    d.   skim through and check for common errors.

I consider a book to be "stellar" when it...
    a.   has relatable characters and a plot that flows.
    b.   highlight's the writer's unique writing style.
    c.   is free of typos.
    d.   is formatted according to *Chicago Manual of Style*.

If you answered mostly **a's**, you are a big picture thinker and you'd make a great **developmental editor**.

If you answered mostly **b's**, you are a **copyeditor** in the making.

If you answered mostly **c's**, you should look into becoming an error-eradicating **proofreader**.

If you answered mostly **d's**, you are on your way to becoming a **style-guide** editing guru.

Let's discuss each type of editing.

*Developmental Editing*
First is developmental editing, which is sometimes referred to as substantive editing. A developmental editor works on the "big picture." Our job starts at the beginning of the publishing process—on a rough draft or even a partial draft. Our concerns include plotline, character development, structure, setting description,

world creation or description, avoiding libel, and the structure of the book's theme.

Some developmental editors read and make comments throughout full drafts of their clients' books. Most often in a Word or Pages document, the "Comments" function is used to suggest edits, additions, and exclusions.

Developmental editors can also take a more "hands-off" approach. Some developmental editors read manuscripts, take notes, and discuss the manuscripts with their clients face-to-face or over some kind of face-to-face communication medium (such as Skype or FaceTime). This hands-off approach works best, in my opinion, for editors who have worked with a client for a number of years on a number of projects and have a clear sense of the author's voice and style.

Another place for developmental editing is in the writing stage; writers often get stuck mid-manuscript and a developmental editor can act as a writing coach to make comments on what the writer has completed so far and offer suggestions for how to move forward. It can take only a small suggestion, like introducing a new character or adding a chapter to further highlight the setting, to get the writing juices flowing again, and developmental editors can be helpful catalysts.

*Copyediting*
Sometimes called "line editing," copyediting begins at the end of the developmental editing stage or when the manuscript reaches a "completed" form. As its alternative name suggests, copyediting means going line-by-line through a manuscript and fixing grammar,

punctuation, spelling, word choice, syntax, flow, and issues with voice.

A good copy editor is able to quickly tune into the author's voice and suggest edits that enhance that voice. Many authors are hesitant to allow an editor to change their writing because too many editors ignore the author's voice and their edits alter that voice. Copy editors need to ask themselves what the author meant to say in each sentence and suggest edits that sound like they came from the author and not the editor. This takes talent and a bit of practice, but you'll know you've got it when a client tells you, "That's what I meant to say! You just said it better than I did."

The most common way to copy edit a manuscript is to use the Track Changes function on Microsoft Word or Pages. I personally prefer to use Microsoft Word, but the Pages software is very similar. Some copy editors will edit by hand on hardcopy manuscripts. While this is doable, it can be cumbersome and time consuming, so keep that in mind when you accept projects in hardcopy. You'll learn how to use Track Changes in chapter 4.

*Proofreading*
Proofreading comes after the formatting stage in book publishing. Proofreaders are the "last eyes" on a manuscript before it goes to print. The proofreader checks a penultimate draft of a book for typos, formatting issues, missing information, and design flaws.

Proofreaders often proof online versions of manuscripts—usually in PDF form. Most self-publishers have a print-on-demand platform connected to an eBook platform. Proofreaders must have a working knowledge of Adobe Acrobat or Adobe PDF reader and be able to mark PDFs in the editing process. Online proofreaders use many of the same "industry" editing marks as do hardcopy proofreaders. If the manuscript is a .doc or .pages, proofreaders can also use Track Changes and the Comments functions to make their edits. I prefer to use this method; the fewer manual changes an author or project editor has to make to a document following a proofreader's edits, the less likely it is that new errors will be introduced to the final publication.

Hardcopy proofreading is, in my experience, growing less and less popular. Hardcopy proofreading requires the proofreader to hand write their edits on a print version of the manuscript. While many argue that hardcopy editing is more thorough than online editing, the hardcopy edits have a better chance of going awry in the final publication than do online edits. Also, doing only hardcopy edits as a proofreader can limit your clientele. You'll be working with local people or only people who will send you their manuscripts through snail mail. Email is instant, and the easier it is for a client to reach you, the better in today's world.

*Style Guide Editing*
Another important type of editing is style guide editing. This is particularly important for academic journals, creative nonfiction, and anything that cites other publications. One of the most popular style guides in the publishing industry is the *Chicago Manual of Style* (*CMOS*). I have used *CMOS* in my work as a contract editor for other editing services companies; I've used *CMOS* to edit PhD dissertations and Master's Theses; I've used *CMOS* to edit creative nonfiction in the

religious studies genre. A working knowledge of the grammar, formatting, and citation rules of *CMOS* is vital for new editors—no matter what kind of services they plan to offer.

A style guide editor does more than fix citation formatting. Guides like *CMOS* dictate rules for correct use of grammar, punctuation, spelling, and even word choice in publications. Style guide editors must have a high level of reading comprehension and recall and must be able to identify and correct sentences that do not adhere to the style rules.

Style guide editors often use Track Changes on online documents and are commonly required to make comments on recurring errors in a book-length manuscript.

My former students called the *CMOS* the "Brick of Knowledge"; if reading the Brick cover-to-cover sounds exciting to you, you might have what it takes to be a style guide guru...and I might pray for you. ;)

## Other Editorial Freelancing Specialties

Freelance editing can encompass a lot more than we talked about above. Many editorial freelancers have experience formatting books or designing cover art. Others are ghostwriters or online content creators. Some organize and manage someone else's online presence as virtual assistants. Here are some of the other services you could offer as an editorial freelancer.

*Formatting*

Formatting—what used to be known as typesetting—is a vital part of the publishing process. In my experience, editors have to master software like Microsoft Word in order to be successful in the self-publishing industry. Platforms like Amazon require formatted Word documents or PDFs exported from Word. Few authors know all of the tricks to getting a book to "look right" or print correctly. I'll be teaching you the keys for formatting in Word in chapter 4.

*Cover Design*

Every book needs an eye-catching cover, and cover designers are the artistic geniuses behind book sales. I know, I know: Never judge a book by its cover. But you know as well as I do that cover design is important in the marketing and sale of books. See chapter 8 to learn how I design basic book covers without a graphic design education. If you're a graphic design genius, you should definitely consider offering a cover design service.

*Ghostwriting*

If you're a gifted writer who can change your writing style to match someone else's voice, ghostwriting might be for you. Ghostwriting is one of my favorite services I offer as The Writing Mechanic. Ghostwriters take the idea and outline of a book and write it for the client. Some copyeditors make good ghostwriters because they can tune into a client's voice and write like their client would write. Ghostwriting requires extensive interviews, research, and a consistent relationship between client and editorial freelancer. If that sounds like the best thing ever, put on your white sheet and get to writing. (I'm funny, I know.)

*Marketing*
When you publish a book, you want it to sell, right? Marketing experts are the puppet masters behind book sales. Amazon is the leading book seller in the world, and many book marketing experts (or publicists, as they are often called) have learned the tricks to selling eBooks and print-on-demand books using Amazon as a catalyst. This is not my particular genius zone (I'm learning!), but many colleges offer marketing classes that would be beneficial for you if you're interested in offering book marketing as part of your freelance editing business. Also look for classes online. I've found some amazing podcasts that dumb the marketing and branding piece down.

*Managing Editors*
Also known as editorial directors, managing editors work for companies that produce a blog or some other kind of consistent online content, have a large email marketing list, distribute newsletters and subscription-based publications, etc. Or they work for specific publications—anthologies or magazines or online content specialists. Managing editors "manage" writers, deadlines, publication schedules, and events while also editing texts and producing email and online content for distribution. If you're particularly organized and driven without needing anyone to push you, you might consider looking for a freelance based (or "remote") managing editor or editorial director position.

*Writing Tutor*
Do you live in a college town or have an "in" with the local school district? Are you really good at helping other people improve their writing? Consider offering tutoring services as part of your freelance business.

University writing centers often hire tutors for their student populations, or you could open an office where you can meet clients and charge an hourly fee to tutor students in writing. This will work best if you are on friendly and professional terms with the local schools; if school officials know you are good at what you do, they will likely be more than willing to refer their students to your services.

*Online Content Creators/Editors—Freelance Writing*
Bloggers, eBook writers, website editors, SEO writers, copywriters: these are all forms of online content creators and editors. Online content creators usually charge by blog/text section or by the word. Many websites and companies hire freelance online content creators/editors to keep up their online presence and further their market reach. A working knowledge of SEO is a big selling point on your resume for these types of positions. You can even become a copywriter for any number of companies or websites that need topic-specific or genre-specific content.

## Caution: Don't Attempt It All

There are so many skills and services you can offer in your freelance editing business, and I hope you can see from these descriptions how your education in the humanities has prepared you to offer them to the publishing market. I hope it is comforting for you to know that the many pages you wrote, the number of red marks and comments you received from your professors on those papers, and the hours you spent reading and editing your peers' work were not for naught. All of that work and attention to detail—all that time spent taking criticism and learning to communicate eloquently—was training you for all of the services you'll be able to offer in your freelance business.

But you can't—or, rather, *shouldn't*—offer all of these services at once. As we will discuss throughout the rest of the book, an important part of building your freelance business is finding your niche: that thing you are interested in and thrive at—your special combination of skills and experience no one else in the world and market has...that thing that makes you the editor you are.

After reading through all those descriptions, I'm guessing a few of them stood out to you immediately and made you say, "Pick me, pick me!" Hone in on those services, and begin planning out what percentage of your business each of the services you want to offer will take.

If you try to offer all of the services I outlined in this chapter, you'll get burned out on freelancing before you even get to the best part: *establishing a client base and working with clients you love and who love you back.*

Trust me: if you offer one service that you love and are energized by and another that you can do but don't like so much, you'll end up spending most of your time on the latter instead of focusing in on the former! Use the worksheet in the appendix to begin planning out your freelance editing business and finding your niche.

Once you decide on the services you want to offer, it's time to start learning necessary software and the specifics of the industry so you can launch your business.

# 3

## What You Need to Know

Freelancers must have at least a basic know-how of various software in order to execute their editing services. I offer in-depth instruction in each of these programs in the following chapters.

### For Text Editing

*Word*

Microsoft Word is THE tool you need in your arsenal. Most of my clients write in Word. Every publishing platform or service I've used requires the interior document to be uploaded as either a Word document or a PDF generated from a Word document. I've taught myself to format books, format graphics and photos, create a live table of contents page, set different headings for each chapter, edit text using Track Changes, compress files, generate different forms of the same document from the Word software, and much, *much* more. In the next chapter, I begin to scratch the surface of the things you need to learn how to do in Word.

*Pages*

Some of your clients will work on a Macintosh computer and won't have Microsoft Word software. I use a MacBook Pro and have downloaded Microsoft Word software, but my computer came with Pages software already loaded. Having immediate and complete access to both Word and Pages software isn't crucial to your editing career, but you may run into a situation, as I did, where Track Changes on Word does not transfer to a Pages document when you save it as a .pages instead of a .doc. It is always easier to edit documents using the software that matches the document form you receive from your client. Therefore, a basic understanding of using Track Changes, comments, and completing basic formatting on Pages software is an important tool to have in your editing toolkit.

*Style Guides*
Chapter 5 is devoted exclusively to style guide editing. Even if you aren't planning to edit academic books, you'll find, as I have, that a general knowledge of popular style guides is vital to your career as an editor. One of my specialties is memoir. Memoir is technically a creative genre, but there are times when memoir authors need to cite sources of some kind—whether it be newspaper articles, other books, or lesser-known events. "Libel" is a terrifying word for memoirists; citing sources—in correct formats according to a well-known style guide—can lower the memoirist's risk of committing libel. Also, style guides are for *much* more than just citations. *The Chicago Manual of Style* ($16^{th}$ edition) has almost 500 pages devoted to editing guidelines for punctuation, spelling, abbreviations, capitalization, grammar, etc. It also contains entire chapters on parts of a book and basic formatting. See chapter 5 for your style guide "how-to."

*Adobe Acrobat*
You may be asked to edit PDFs, and Adobe Acrobat is a free, easy-to-use software for PDF editing. There are

tons of add-on tools for Adobe Acrobat—all of which you have to pay for—but the basic highlighting, commenting, and adding text tools are included in the free download. Finding where those basic tools live is the most difficult part of learning the software.

*Editing Marks*
While this obviously isn't a kind of "software," copyeditors and proofreaders should know the generally accepted editing marks. Most of your projects nowadays will be on the computer, but you will occasionally come across one in hard copy. See Appendix A for where to download the list of editing marks.

## For Cover Design

*Canva*
Canva is an online design platform that is user friendly and allows editors like me to create beautiful cover designs and eBooks quickly and easily. Using Canva, you can create eye-catching cover designs for print-on-demand and eBook and design and download complete eBook documents for upload to Kindle Direct Publishing or instant PDF download. You can create blog graphics, Pinterest graphics, social media post graphics, descriptive graphics—I've even used it to create diagrams for workbooks. There is a free version available, but if you're serious about your design game as a freelancer—and if you plan to offer any kind of self-publishing services—you should purchase the paid, business version. Learn how to use Canva to create a cover design in chapter 8.

*InDesign*
Many publications use InDesign to format publications and create cover designs. InDesign can seem like a complex system, and it is in many ways, but once you locate and learn the basic functions, you've made it. After mastering the basics, learning InDesign is about Googling instructions on how to perform a specific function for a particular project. You won't know (nor do you need to know) how to execute every function in InDesign, but when a need arises, you will be able to figure out how to accomplish it for your client in InDesign with the basic rules mastered. I will not be teaching you how to use InDesign in this book. I paid a monthly fee to have InDesign on my computer for a few years, but the more I learn about using Word, the more easily I can use Word (and Canva) to completely replace InDesign in my editing work. We'll talk about that.

## Online Services

*Basic Website Design*
This was bane of my editorial existence in the first few years, but I would grit my teeth and push through on tech support live chats and help-ticket email exchanges and Google how-to's to design and use my website when it was a WordPress website. SquareSpace is a-floppity-jillion-times more user friendly than WordPress. SquareSpace offers a visual page builder that is fun and simple to navigate and build with. Plus, SquareSpace costs a lot less! A yearly fee for a "Personal" website with SquareSpace is $144. You'll be hard pressed to find a WordPress host that costs less than $200 per year. (And in case you're wondering, no, I don't get paid to promote SquareSpace. I just love it that much.)

Now, I am not a techy person by nature. I edit books with words and few acronyms. I still honestly couldn't explain what a DNS setting is or what it does, and I sure as heck can't ever explain how plugins work. But learning as much as I needed in order to build a website for my own business enabled me to offer advice to my clients looking to start their author websites or asking me to build a basic one for them. Like so much of the more extraneous software I have listed here as "need-to-know" for working as a freelance editor, just learn the basics and you'll do fine. We "life-long-learners" are good at that sort of thing, remember? We'll go over designing an author website for your clients and designing and utilizing a website for your freelance business.

*Self-Publishing Platforms*
The most popular eBook self-publishing platform (and the one I use and suggest my authors use) is Amazon Kindle Direct Publishing. In addition, Amazon's print-on-demand company allows you to create a paper-back book and eBook version of the book on the largest book selling network in the world. As editors, you need to learn the ropes of Amazon Kindle Direct Publishing, including formatting specifics and document types required for each book format, so that you can assist your authors. You'll hear me say it again and again: the publishing world is moving toward self-publishing! As a new freelance editor, you need to place yourself at the head of the pack in acquiring the skills and knowledge necessary to be of service to your authors. And those skills are in self-publishing.

*Social Media*
Surely you know (or you'll know by the end of this book) the value of social media for your own work and personal

brand, but authors need to have social media accounts to build their readerships and following and sell their books. As an editor, knowing social media best practices for popular platforms and being able to create and build networks for your authors will serve as a highly coveted and marketable skill in your editing arsenal.

In the next chapters, we will dig into each skill and build up your knowledge and know-how so you can become a desired editor-for-hire.

# 4

## Word? Word.

We use Word for words. Go figure. Word will be your most-used software in your freelance editing career (assuming you're editing text as your primary service). In this chapter we will explore the most common and necessary functions of Word for your editing services.

*Track Changes*
Up first is the function that will let you make and show your edits: Track Changes. This function is found under your Review tab. Some versions have a button that you have to select to turn the function on; others have a digital slide that will turn green when its engaged. There is also a dropdown box with options like "simple markup," "final," "all markup," "no markup," or "original." Your version of Word may have other titles for these options, but the basic functions are the same.

Also in the Track Changes tab is a "Markup Options" button or dropdown box. There you can select how you view the edits. You can have everything show up in the text itself ("Show all revisions inline") or "show revisions in balloons." There is also an option in the Review tab to select "Reviewing," which will show the review pane to the left of the document. I prefer NOT to select the review pane because as you add edits with Track Changes on, the review pane will fill up and it tends to slow down your document performance. (Curse you, rainbow wheel of death!)

The rest of the buttons in the Track Changes tab are for accepting, rejecting, or viewing the next or previous change in the document. I'll take you through how and when to use each button or option in the example below.

So let's pretend we are starting a new manuscript edit. We pull up the document in Word and go to the Review tab. Before you begin any editing work, turn on Track Changes. In the drop down box, select "simple markup." Then, as you go through and delete text, add text, or move text, you'll notice red lines that show up in either the left or right margin next to the lines you edit (The side the red line is on depends on whether or not your document is formatted with mirrored margins. We'll talk about that when we go over formatting in Word). If you click on one of the lines, the Track Changes function will switch to "all markup" and you'll see text underlined or crossed out in the document and/or balloons in the comments pane (which will show up on the right side of the document). The screen shots below are from my software. I currently use Microsoft Word 2016. If you use the 2010 or 2013 versions, your review tab and Track Changes options might look a little different, but you, my life-long learners, should be able to figure out the different options based on my descriptions of what each option does in the following photos. If you can't—and you have been searching on the Google-box for an extensive amount of time in attempt to figure it out on your own but are striking out—take some screen shots of your software options and email them to me with your questions: thewritingmechanic@gmail.com.

## Track Changes:

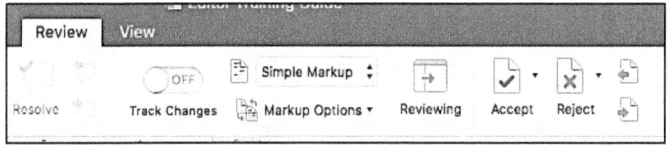

Slide the button over to turn Track Changes on, or press the button.

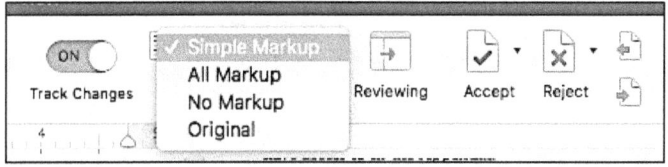

With Track Changes now turned on, go to the dropdown box and select Simple Markup. Your version of Word might say "Basic Markup."

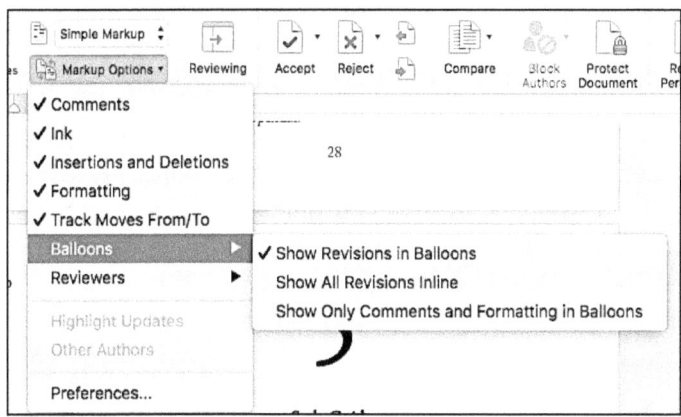

Then, view the Markup options and see how your edits will be shown when you switch to "All Markup." I generally choose the "Show Revisions in Balloons option.

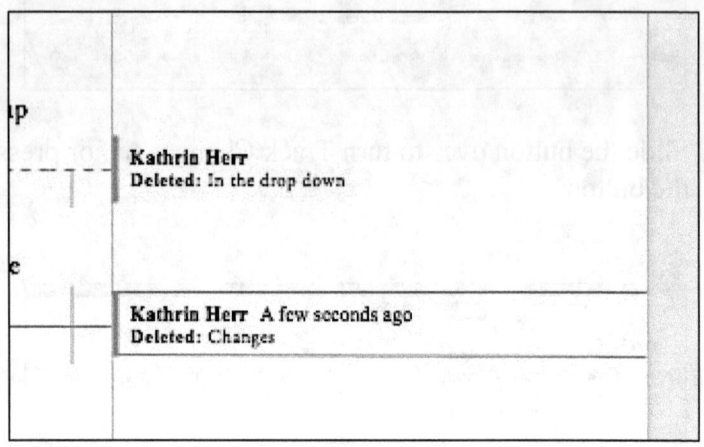

With the balloons function, your edits will show up in the right pane.

If you choose the "show all revisions in line" option, your edits will show up like the above photo. Text with a line through it is text you deleted; underlined text is text you added. When you move text in a sentence or paragraph, you will see both the crossed out and underlined sections of text in the in line revisions when you switch to All Markup.

Here are a few tips for using Track Changes:
1. If you need to change a few letters in the middle of a word, it will be less confusing for your client

viewing your edits on "all markup" if you delete the whole word and add the corrected word.
2. If you are working with footnotes and need to move the footnote number to the end of the sentence, turn Track Changes off to move it and then make a comment to indicate that you turned TC off to do that. If you leave TC on, the number will show up as adding an additional footnote because the number you deleted will not disappear entirely. It will still be in the "all markup" version of the document.
3. You may need to do a "find and replace all" for double spaces after periods in a manuscript. You may also need to change all of the quotation marks to either curly or straight depending on the style you're going for (*CMOS* is specific about this). To do fixes like that (where the number of changes can be in the thousands) turn TC off, make the change, and then make a comment either at the beginning of the manuscript or in your editor's letter.
4. If you move an entire paragraph or multiple sentences of text in the manuscript with TC turned on, you will not be able to show your line-by-line edits. The entire text will show that it has been deleted and then added elsewhere. Follow the same process as for the other points above: turn TC off, move the paragraph, turn TC back on to make your edits, and make a comment on the paragraph showing where you moved it from and why.
5. I also suggest you turn Track Changes off when you move or delete photos or graphics. Leaving Track Changes on when you move or delete photos and graphics can make the document size

enormous, which will frustrate the heck out of you when you try to do anything else with it.
6. When you get to the end of your editing process and send the edited document back to your author, check the document size in your document folder. If the Track Changes made the document too large to email, consider uploading it into Google Drive (which is free with a free Gmail account) and share the document link with your client via email. Make sure you indicate that anyone with the link "can edit" the document, not just view it. That way your author will be able to download the document.
7. When you send the document back to your author, instruct them to view the book in "Final" or "Simple Markup" view before they go edit by edit. When you're copyediting, an important aspect is how you were able to improve the flow of the text with your edits. Make sure they read through the sentences with your edits in place (not showing) before they see exactly how you changed the sentence. It can be overwhelming for authors to see all of the edits to their text at once. They'll think they stink at writing if they see all the red all over the book they worked so hard to write.

*Comments*

Another essential function of Word is the Comments function. You can add comments to anything in the main body of the text. Use comments to make note of common errors, style guide rules, explanations for particular edits, etc. You can add comments to text in a few ways:

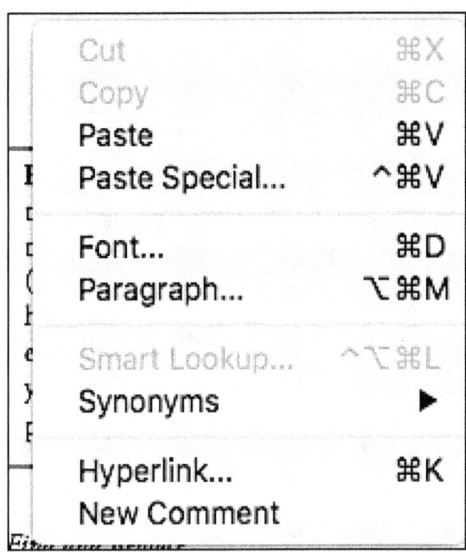

You can right click and select "New Comment."

Or go back to the Review tab. After highlighting the text, select "New Comment" to add your comment.

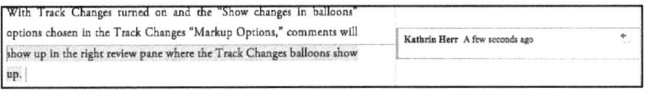

With the "Show changes in balloons" options chosen in the Track Changes "Markup Options," comments will show up in the right pane where the Track Changes balloons show up.

> Or, go back to the Review tab. After highlighting [KH1]text, select "New Comment" to add your comment. [KH2]

With the "Show changes in line" option chosen in the Track Changes "Markup Options," comments will show up in the text and will appear in the Review pane to the left of the document when that is chosen.

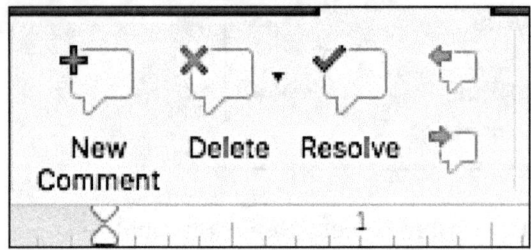

Use the rest of the buttons in the Review tab to go to the next comment or previous comment in the document, delete comments or "resolve" them. The bottom icon on the right takes you to the next comment, and the top icon on the right takes you to the previous comment. You can click the "Delete" icon to delete one comment, or go to the drop down arrow to delete all comments in the document:

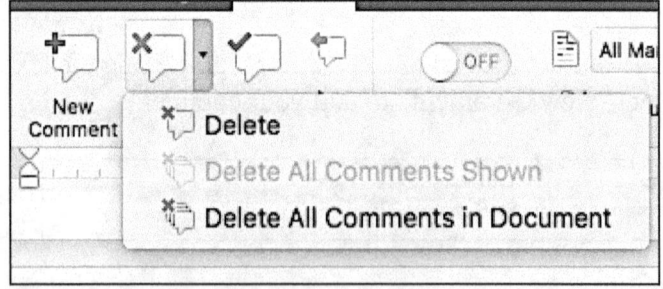

You can also right click in the comment and select delete, reply to, or resolve the comment.

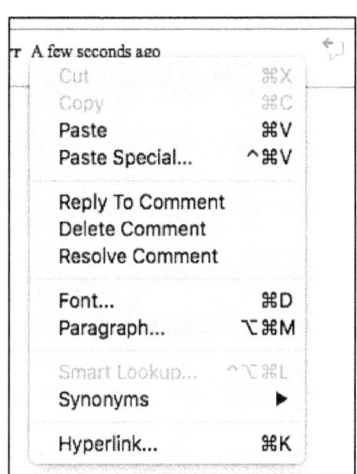

You can reply to comments other people make or to your own comments in a text by clicking the icon with the purple arrow to the right of the comment bubble:

When you reply to a comment, you will see two layers—one for the original comment and one for the reply:

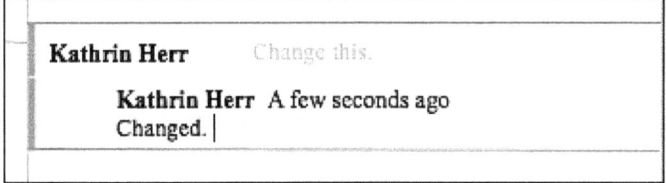

You can also "Resolve" comments. The resolving option is great for documents that go through multiple edits with multiple contributors. When you "resolve" a comment, it will remain in the document but will be faded:

> **Kathrin Herr** A few seconds ago
> Change this.

In my experience, comments are the most useful to help explain your edits to your clients (supplemental or taking the place of your editor's letter) and to make note of sections of text your author needs to complete or continue to develop.

**Warning!** If you have Track Changes turned off when you add comments and then delete them with Track Changes turned on, they will remain in the Review pane. Then, we you try to go from one comment to the next using the arrows, your document will get hung up on the deleted comment that is still there in the Review pane. It's a pain in the behind, so try to avoid that.

> **Editing Tip**: As you make your way through the text, add comments to errors you come across regularly. Then, when you are going through your final checks, use the find and replace function (explained next) to make changes for consistency of use. No matter how careful you are with your editing, you are bound to miss repeated errors when you're editing a 200-page book. Adding comments can allow you time to double check your consistency before you submit the project to your client.

*Find and Replace*
The find and replace function is essential for full-length book manuscript edits—particularly in copyediting and proofreading. It can be difficult for editors to stay consistent in longer manuscripts. The find and replace function allows you to make sure you fix all common, recurring errors and double check punctuation, capitalization, and other errors in formatting. You can search for almost anything in the "Find and Replace" function. As long as you can find the right combination to search for in the document, you can check and edit every instance of an error in any length book.

In Word for Mac, which is what I use on my MacBook Pro, the search bar is on the top right side of the document. An easy way to find the search bar is to hit Command+F or Control+F—depending on your computer system. You can type your search terms into the box and hit enter and they will be highlighted in the text. However, it is more efficient if you get them to show up in the left sidebar. You can choose that option in the top right-hand box by clicking the dropdown arrow or in the View tab by selecting "Navigation Pane":

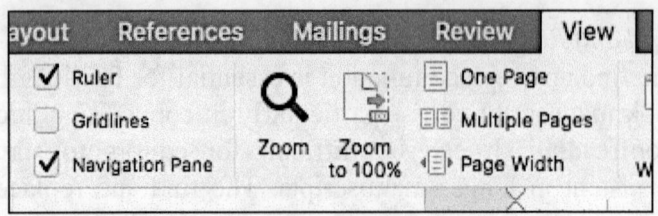

Once you get the Navigation pane on, you'll see two input bars: one for the search terms and one for the replacement text.

When you type in the search terms, the matches will be highlighted in the text. Click "Find" to go from match to match. The drop down boxes contain types of text you can search for or replace text with.

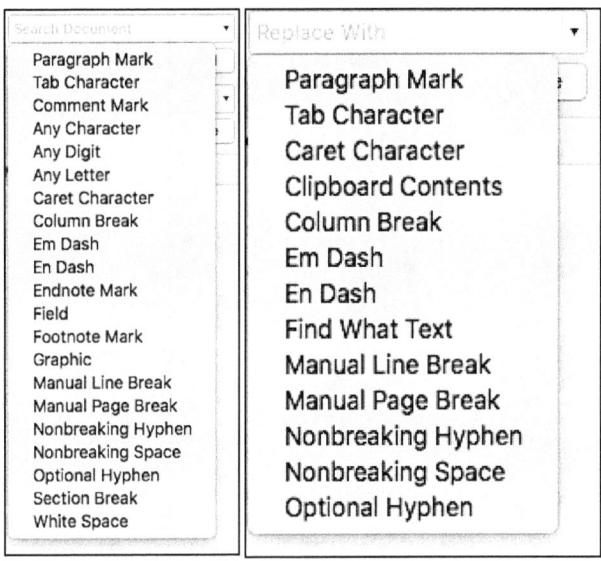

There is also a settings button with options for how the program will recognize the search term you put in the Search bar:

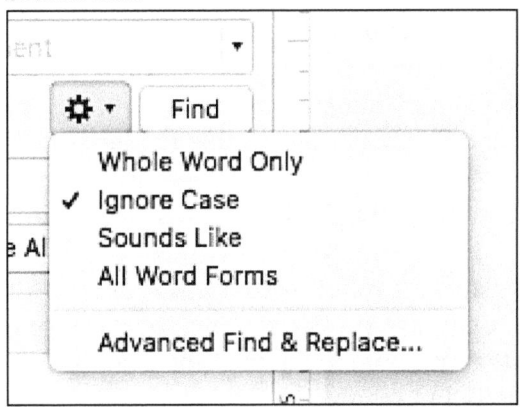

For even more options, click the "Advanced Find & Replace" option to view this window:

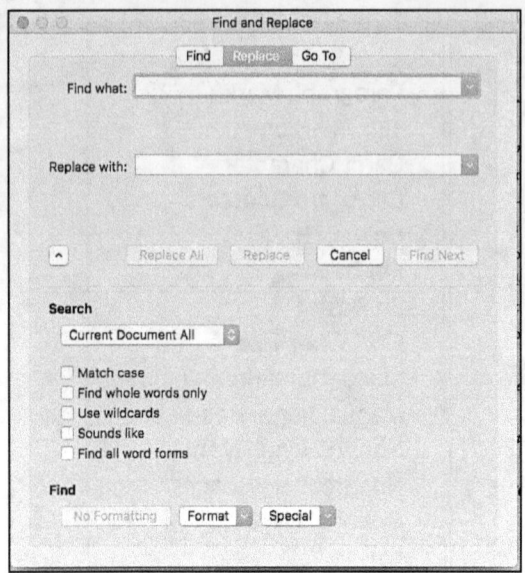

If the bottom section doesn't show up when you open the Advanced window, select the arrow (shown on the right middle side of the window pictured). I suggest you pull up a book manuscript and mess around with the various Format, Special, Search Document, Replace With, and all other options in the Find & Replace window and side pane to discover everything you are able to search for.

Some tips for using Find & Replace for editing manuscripts:
1. Be extremely careful with the "Replace All" button. Only use it for errors that occur a lot or errors that are not situational. For example, use Replace All to remove all double spaces (search for two spaces and replace with one space), but do not use Replace All to fix errors in the usage of the word "which."
2. Keep Track Changes turned on when you're using Find and Replace unless you're fixing an

error that would require the use of the "Replace All" button. That way, if you accidentally replace something incorrectly, you can "reject" the change and correct it.
3. If you're looking for something specific, like the way in which an author uses a particular term throughout the text, search narrowly to broadly. Start by searching for the exact word in the exact case, format, and style you're checking for. For example, if you're looking to see whether an author capitalizes the words "He," "Him, and "His" when referring to God, search for space+He+space and uncheck the "Ignore case" option in the settings. Then, if you need to edit capitalization of He, Him, and His search instead for space+God+space and read each sentence where the word "God" appears, as well as the paragraph surrounding each instance. This will be more efficient than searching for space+he+space because there may be hundreds of other times when the author refers to a male entity that is not the God that is most often referred to using masculine pronouns.
4. Many authors accidentally input "styles" to various sections of their text that increase the size of the manuscript and mess up the Live Table of Contents generation. Below you'll learn how to introduce Styles to headers for a Live TOC, but **before** you remove styles formatting by selecting the entire text (with Track Changes turned off!) and clicking "remove formatting" or "normal" in the styles list, with the find & replace function, search for all italicized text. Taking the styles formatting off will remove all italicized text, and you want to make sure you indicate what was

italicized to yourself so you can put it back in italics after you remove the formatting. So, go to the advanced options in the find and replace window, click the "Format" dropdown box and select font. Then select "Italic" in the Font Style dropdown box. The document will highlight all the italic text. Scroll through each section of italic text and highlight it or change the font color in some way. See the screen shots below:

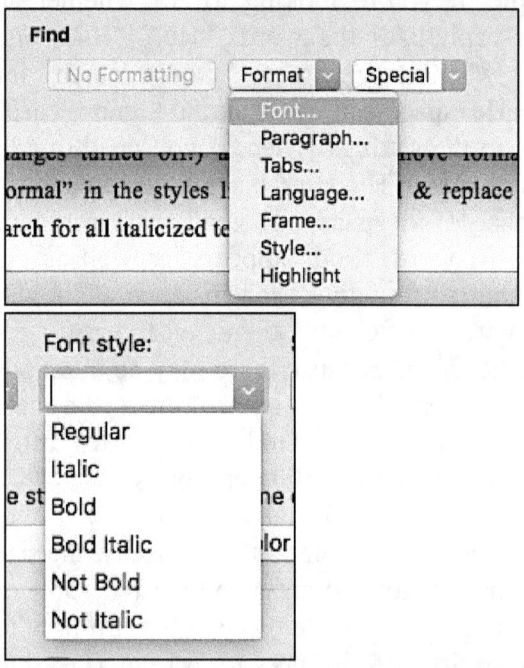

*Page Setup*
If you're using Amazon to publish your book, you'll need to know how to alter page size, margins, gutter position, and how to create "mirrored margins" in your documents. We will go into more detail in about the

specifics of formatting, but here is a general overview of where to find the page setup functions in Word.

While you can simply go to the Layout tab at the top of the page—where you'll see margins, orientation, size, etc. as options—I suggest that you instead go to the Format menu and click Document.

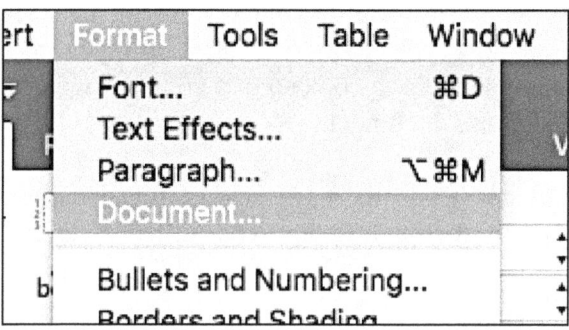

You will then see this window:

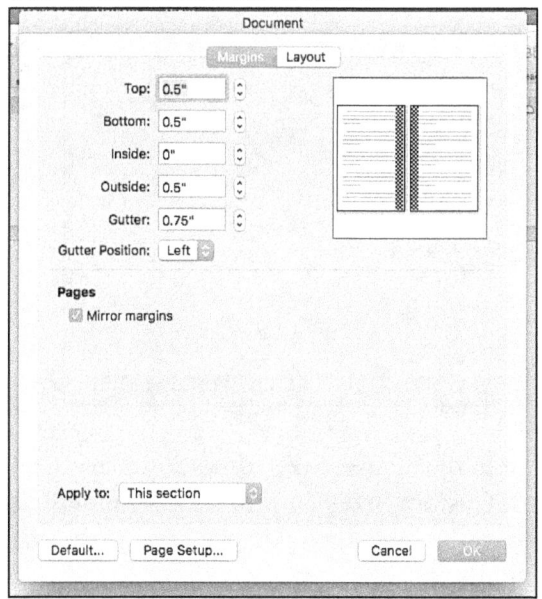

If you do not need to change the size of your document (the automatic page size is 8.5"x11"), you can adjust your margins in this window. Notice a few things: First, if you have "Mirrored Margins" selected, you will need to verify that your "Gutter Position" is correct. Choose left if you're formatting a book for print. Also, notice that the drop down box toward the bottom of the window says "Apply to: This Section." If your document has more than one section, you want to make sure you have "Whole Document" in the box so that your changes will apply to the entire document.

If you need to change the page size of the document, click the button for Page Setup. You will then see this window:

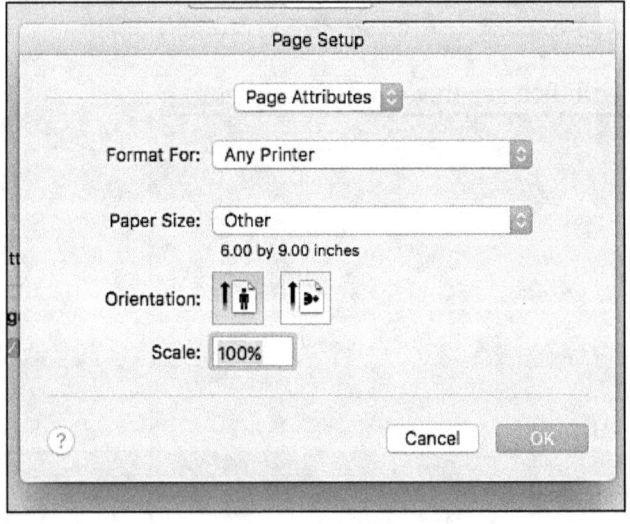

From there, go to the "Paper Size" drop down menu and click "Manage Custom Sizes." From there, you will see the following window in which you can change the page width and height.

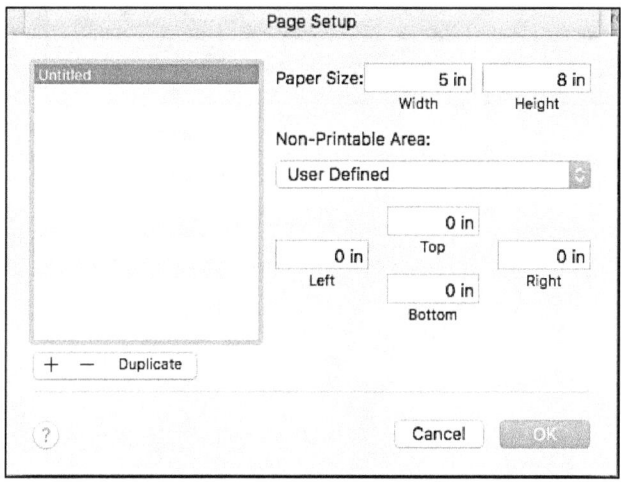

Also notice that you can adjust the Non-Printable Area. I suggest you keep your desired margin sizes in mind and adjust the non-printable area accordingly. For my book, I have the non-printable area set to zero. My margins, then, are half-inch on all sides, with the gutter set to .75" with mirrored margins. Your document might be different depending on what you're formatting the document for.

*Formatting*

Other kinds of formatting you must know how to do in Word for your editing business include styles, section breaks, unique headers, and page number formatting.

Text styles are important for navigation in a document and for creating live contents tables. In your "Home" tab, you should see a window with various styles, such as "Normal," "Heading 1," "Heading 2," etc. You'll use the various heading styles for your chapter titles or sections within particular chapters.

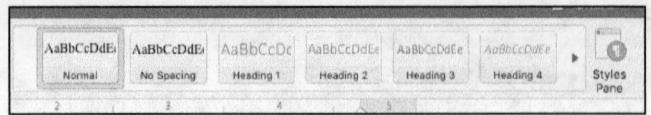

You can also click "Styles Pane" for more options:

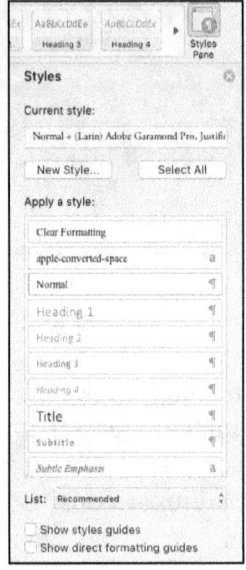

I tend to use "Heading 2" for my chapter titles when I'm formatting a book if I'm not including any section headers in the Table of Contents. If you need to set multiple page headers in the same format, create a new style. I base most of my chapter headings off of "Heading 2" and adjust the font, font size, and any others. Make sure you select "Add to Quick Style list" at the bottom of the window for ease of formatting.

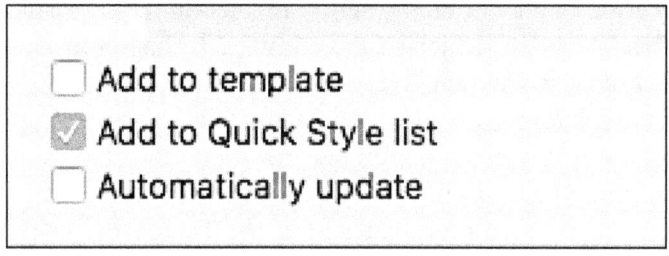

Then, when you highlight the chapter tiles and select the style, your chapter heading will show up in your navigation on the left side of the screen when "Navigation Pane" is selected in the View tab.

Another main kind of formatting you'll need to know how to do is to create sections. Go to the Layout tab and look for the "Breaks" dropdown box:

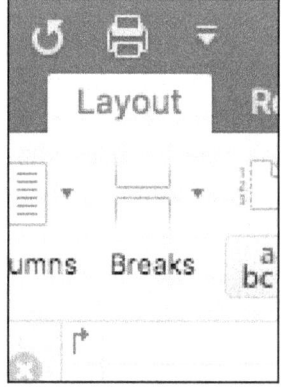

In that menu, you'll see a number of options in two sections, Page Breaks and Section Breaks. In general, you'll need to utilize the "Next Page" option under Section Breaks. Adding a section break for "Next Page" means wherever your cursor is in the text, a section break will show up at the top of the page following that location. You can input section breaks on the last pages of each chapter, which would allow each chapter to stand as a unique "section." Having different sections allows you to change your running headers and footers text and to adjust your page number position and inclusion. Section breaks allow you to dictate that the page number will only show up on pages after the Table of Contents or the rest of the front matter of the book. They can also allow you to choose different headers on odd or even pages to reflect the chapter title for each section.

> **Tip for Formatting in Word**: In the home tab, find and select this icon: ¶. Your document will show all non-printed characters: your spaces, hard returns, section and page breaks, and any other formatting in the text. Selecting the ¶ icon allows you to make sure your section breaks are in the correct places in the text so that your headers don't end up wonky. It is also a good idea to select this icon right when you get a document from a client so that you can see what formatting already exists. You'll save yourself time and frustration upfront if you fix the formatting issues before you start editing.

To adjust your headers and footers, then, simply double click in either the header or footer of a section you're wanting to edit. The Header/Footer tab will appear next to your last tab at the top of the document:

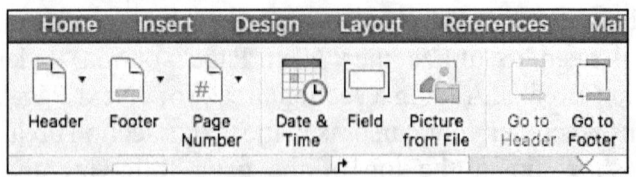

There are a number of options for headers and footers. Let's start at the far left. Under the Header and Footer icons are a number of predetermined header and footer style options. You can mess around with those styles in your documents to find one that works for you or your client or you can format and style your own. To the right of that is the Page Number icon.

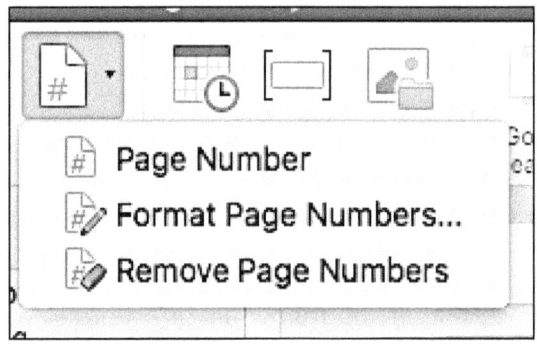

In order to "Format Page Numbers" you have to first add page numbers by clicking Page Number.

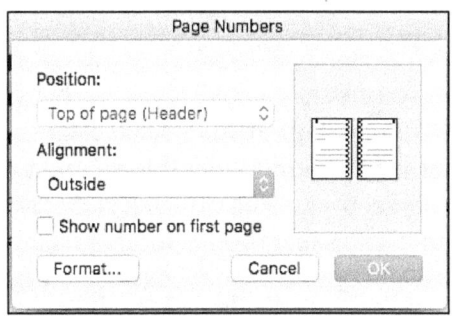

You can determine where you would like to show the page number in the window that pops up. Then, you can format your page numbers in the "Page Number Format" window. Notice that you can adjust the number format, and choose whether to continue page numbering from the previous section or to start at a number of your choosing at the start of that particular section:

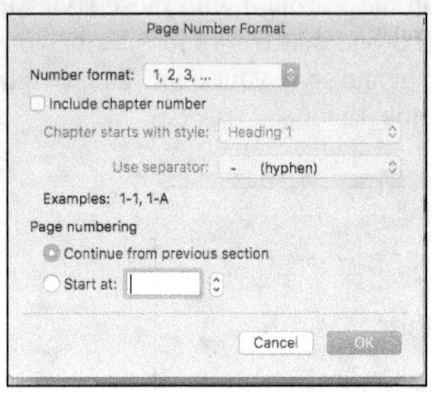

\*\*For some advanced formatting, select the "Include chapter number" option and follow the directions in the popup message window.\*\*

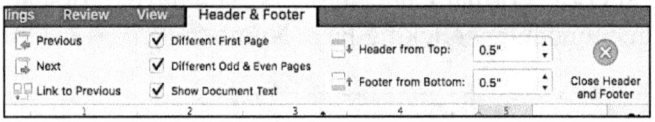

You can see in the screen-shot above that the button "Link to Previous" is not highlighted. That means that the section my cursor is in will not link all formatting of headers to the previous section format. If I select that and change the header in a later section, I will also change the header in the earlier sections. *Always* unselect "Link to Previous" when you format headers in a document with multiple sections. Moving to the right, you'll use the two top options, "Different First Page" and "Different Odd & Even Pages," a lot when you're formatting books. The "Different First Page" option means the first page of every new section will have a different header and footer than the rest of the pages in that particular section. Books often do not show a page number or header on the first page of each chapter. Selecting the "Different First Page" option will allow you to adjust the formatting to account for that. The next option, "Different Odd & Even Pages," is for if you want to show the title of the book or the author name on even numbered pages and the chapter titles on odd numbered pages. The last option in the Header & Footer tab allows you to dictate how far from the top or bottom of the page your header/footer will appear. Keep your "Non-Printable Area" specifications in mind from your document set up when you dictate your header/footer distance. The bottom option is only for how your document appears when you're in the header/footer tab. If you unselect "Show Document Text," the text in the regular document will disappear from view.

When you have more than one section in your document, selecting your header/footer area will show the section number you'll be editing if you add or delete anything from the header/footer section highlighted:

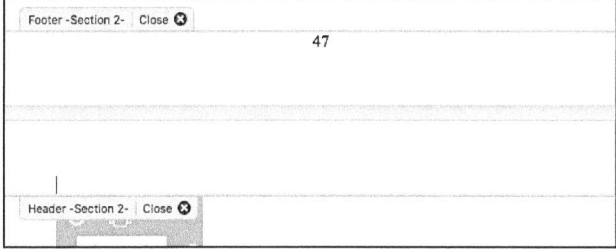

Some tips on using section breaks for formatting of headers/footers:
1. Always turn Track Changes *off* to add section breaks and adjust header/footer formatting.

Tracking formatting changes like that can make your document enormous and slow it down—or even crash it out, which will give you about 20 minutes of heart-dropping, face-palming agony. Trust me.
2. Follow the tip above and select the ¶ icon in the home tab to view your section break locations. There may be a time when you need to delete a section break. With the ¶ icon selected, you can see and highlight the section break and then delete it from the document.
3. Be careful when you double click in the header of a particular section that the document doesn't jump to another section to show the header/footer. Keep track of the section you're in and make sure it says the correct section number (i.e., "Header - Section X") before you go about making changes.
4. Save often when adding and formatting headers/footers. The added code can cause Word to crash, and take it from me: it is *devastating* to have a document crash after hours of formatting work when you haven't saved it. Don't waste your time. Save as often as you can. (Command+S = Your best short code pal!)

*Live TOCs*
A Live Table of Contents is vital to your eBook formatting service. We'll talk more about eBook formatting, but here is a quick overview of how to create a live TOC in word. When you're on the page toward the beginning of the document where you want to add your TOC, go to the References tab at the top of the document and select the Table of Contents icon. A box with style options will drop down and you can select a premade

TOC format or create your own. If you've given each chapter a heading style (and made sure your TOC will show those specific styles), your TOC will be populated with the text of each chapter title and will indicate the page number it is located on. If you make edits to the text following the addition of the TOC, right click in the table (or click the arrow at the top of the TOC to show the dropdown box) and select "Update Field." You can then choose whether you want to update only the page numbers of the TOC or to update the text also. If you've made any changes to the chapter titles, you must have the TOC update the entire table.

Tips:
1. Turn Track Changes off to add a live TOC and to update the TOC.
2. Be careful when clicking around in the table after it is created. Clicking on a chapter title will take you to the first page of that chapter. If you want to change the font, click and hold and drag your cursor to highlight the text you want to change.

Now let's start digging into the specific services you may want to offer to your clients in your freelance editing business. I'll be going into a lot of detail on the particular formatting specifications for the platforms you'll most likely use in your business to publish print and eBooks for your clients, but first, here is an overview of the editing service tailor-made for the most detail-oriented editors: style guide editing.

# 5

## Style Guides

There are many style guides you might need to learn to use as a freelance editor. Once you learn one style guide well and figure out what basic things to look out for, you'll be able to learn to work with any style guide.

The key to learning a style guide is knowing where your most valuable educational resources are located online and in print. I include the Purdue Online Writing Lab online resources because OWL offers the most succinct explanation of citation rules for each manual of style used in academic work (*MLA, APA, AP, CMOS* ). It is incredibly useful for learning to format citations in footnotes, endnotes, and basic paper structure:

*MLA*
Humanities schools and publications require the use of the *Modern Language Association* (*MLA*) style formatting and editing.

*MLA* website: https://www.mla.org/
Purdue Online Writing Lab (OWL) MLA resources link:
    https://owl.english.purdue.edu/owl/resource/747/01/
*MLA* Print Edition: http://amzn.to/2jRp5w1

*APA*
Editing for the social sciences will often require the use of the *American Psychological Association* (*APA*) style formatting and editing.

*APA* website: http://www.apa.org/
Purdue OWL *APA* resources link:
    https://owl.english.purdue.edu/owl/resource/560/01/
*APA* Print Edition: http://amzn.to/2kcT95S

    \*\*Here is an APA cheat sheet I've used: https://www.codot.gov/business/grants/safetygrants/documents/APStyleGuideCheatSheet.pdf

*AP*
Journalists adhere to the *Associated Press* (AP) style guide.

*AP* website: http://www.apstylebook.com/
Purdue OWL *AP* resources link:
    https://owl.english.purdue.edu/owl/resource/735/02/
*AP* Print Edition: http://amzn.to/2knxxWN


*Christian Writer's Manual of Style*
A specific style guide I've used for religious studies editing and popular Christian publications is the *Christian Writer's Manual of Style*. Written by Robert Hudson, the *CWMS* uses *Chicago* style as a baseline for its rules and adds rules for capitalization, spelling,

punctuation, abbreviation, hyphenation, etc., that are used in religious studies publications specifically.

Christian Writer's Manual of Style Book on Amazon:
http://amzn.to/2kndzM0

*CMOS*

The most commonly used style guide in the freelance editing world—and the one I recommend you learn as thoroughly as you can—is the *Chicago Manual of Style* (*CMOS*). You can get a print edition of the "Brick of Knowledge" online or in most bookstores. *CMOS* also has an online subscription service that allows you to search for specific rules in the guide. However, if you purchase the *CMOS* print edition and learn to use the table of contents and the index, you'll be nearly as efficient as the online subscription (without the yearly subscription bill). However, I recommend you update your *CMOS* print library every few years to keep up with the most recent, thorough edition.

## Learning the *CMOS* TOC & Index

Always use the index rule: search narrow first and then broaden the parameters; then, once you find the correct section, start to narrow in on your question again. Once you get the hang of the basic structure of the *CMOS*, you'll be able to go straight to specific chapters to find what you're looking for.

For example, if you had a question about whether a word used in a specific religious practice is capitalized, you would start out looking for that word in the index. You'd find it didn't have a listing, and you'd broaden your search to "capitalization." Looking then in the TOC, you'd search for a section on capitalization. You'd see quickly that chapter 8, "Names and Terms," is a 100-page section on capitalization. Then, narrowing in again, you'd find the subtitle, "Religious Events, Concepts, Services, and Objects 8.107," and turning to that section, you'd discover the rule on whether to capitalize the word you were wondering about.

Another example: Say you come across an instance where an author spells out the days of the week in some places and abbreviates them in others. You know from your training that consistency is vital, so you have to figure out what *CMOS* says about abbreviating days of the week. You'd start your search in the index for "abbreviating days of the week." You'd look under "A" and see that though there is a two column section on abbreviation, "days of the week" is not an option listed there. Then, you'd search for "days of the week." The entry in the Index says, "days of the week, 8.87, 10.41. *See also dates*." Now, you know already that chapter 8 is almost exclusively rules about capitalization, so you'd look past the 8.87 rule to the 10.41 rule. Upon seeing "*See also dates*," you'd look at the listing for "dates," under which reads, "abbreviations: days of the week, 10.41." Bingo! Going then to chapter 10, you would find rules for abbreviating days of the week.

Finding a rule in the *CMOS* index is sort of like searching the Google-sphere for some remote concept; you have to think of every possible word to use for that concept and begin searching. You don't know which version of your search will yield the correct results until you learn the system you're working with. Eventually, you'll know the *CMOS* backwards and forwards and be able to skip the index and go straight to a specific chapter, find the section, learn the rule, and make your edits faster than you can say, "Brick of Knowledge."

*CMOS* website:
> http://www.chicagomanualofstyle.org/

Purdue OWL *CMOS* resources link:
> https://owl.english.purdue.edu/owl/resource/717/03/

*CMOS* Print Edition: http://amzn.to/2knmSM3

*In-House Style Guides*
Aside from the main market style guides listed above, individual publications or publishing entities may dictate their own style guide with rules that cover topics specific to their publication(s). In-house style guides will provide you with the formatting basics, software preferences and protocols, and they usually give copyeditors a guide with rules about hyphenation, abbreviation, capitalization, and punctuation.

Many in-house style guides are based on an established style guide. If they pull from a guide like the *CMOS*, the editors will usually provide copy editors with a document that shows which *CMOS* rules they adhere to and which rules they alter for their publication(s). I've found many in-house style guides pull from *CMOS*, so as long as you know *CMOS* style and use any documents the editors give you as a reference, you'll catch onto in-house style guides quickly.

**Tip**: Read through the in-house style guide before starting any editing project for a particular publishing entity and then skim through it every time you restart the project. I like to scan the in-house style guide every time I open the document to edit to refresh myself on the specifics of that particular publishing entity.

**Tip**: Use the comments function to your advantage in the style guide editing process. Every time you make a style guide edit to a text, comment on it with a note to yourself to search for that error in the rest of the document upon completion of the first round of edits. That will allow you to check yourself at the end to make sure you didn't miss any repeated errors.

Once the book is edited, the next step is publishing. Next, let's talk about how to get books ready for publication through print-on-demand and eBook platforms.

# 6

## Self-Publishing

You'll hear me say it over and over again: self-publishing is your golden ticket to the freelance editing world. There could not have been a better market shift for freelancers than the shift from majority traditional publishing to majority self-publishing. Websites like Amazon are huge and hugely successful in selling books for a reason. They make it easy for authors to publish and sell their books online.

What is also great about the burgeoning popularity of self-publishing for freelancers like us is the way in which authors and readers are beginning to recognize the value in editing for self-published books. Readers are realizing they don't want to read poorly edited books, and authors are realizing they don't to present sloppy writing to their readers. This is where we swoop in to save the day.

But we can't simply know grammar rules and writing mechanics and expect to be successful in the field of editorial freelancing when the market is becoming more and more constituted by self-publishers. We need to learn the self-publishing world and be able to guide our authors through the maze from first draft to a sellable book.

In this chapter, I give you all the knowhow you need to use the most popular self-publishing platform in the country for print-on-demand.

*Self-Publishing on Amazon KDP*
Kindle Direct Publishing is where self-publishers who want to sell on Amazon go to get the print version of their books printed and an eBook of the same book. It is a fairly user-friendly platform with a free account signup and step-by-step processes to help authors successfully publish their books for print-on-demand.

However, most authors don't have time (or desire) to learn how to size their interior documents, design their covers, calculate spine size, and ensure that headers and page numbers are correct in the document. They don't want to be concerned with margins and exporting the correct document format. They want to give someone else their manuscript, sit back, and have a professional editor/designer make it into a book. That is why the paid editing and design services are so appealing to authors.

Because the paid editing services option is available, you as a freelancer need to learn all of the specifics for publishing a book using the KDP platform so an author can come to you for the complete editing and publishing package instead.

*Page Set-up for Interior Documents*
First thing's first: here's how to set up a book for print-on-demand. KDP offers 16 different page sizes for books they print in-house and make available for sale on Amazon. The most common are 5.25"x8", 5.5"x8.5", 6"x9", 7"x10", 8"x10", 8.25"x6", 8.25"x8.25", 8.5"x11". The standard page sizes come with pre-set

cover design templates on their website. However, I've used 5"x8", 5.25"x8", 5.5"x8.5", 6"x9", and 8.5"x11" for my clients over the years, and I've found that it is simpler to learn the basic formatting principles for the interior documents and cover design set up for the four book sizes I've used the most than to rely on the KDP software to set it up for me.

Let's use the 5"x8" page size as our example. I like the 5x8 size for creative books like novels and memoirs, and I always suggest using 5x8 or 5.25"x8.25" for books in my niche. Flip back in chapter 4 where I demonstrated how to set up the page size in the Format menu at the top of the document. In the "Manage custom sizes" window, you will change the document to 5x8. Also, make sure the Non-Printable Area is User Defined, and set the non-printable area to 0 all around. Then, we need to think about margin size, mirrored margins, and gutter position.

Think about a print book format (take this one for example!). You need a slightly larger margin where the pages are bound in the spine so you don't have any text folded into the spine and cutting it off. The way to avoid that issue to set up the document with mirrored margins and a "gutter" that is slightly larger than the margins you set. In this case, with a page size of 5x8, I have all margins other than the inside set to .5" inches, I have the mirrored margins option checked, and I have the gutter position on the left at .75".

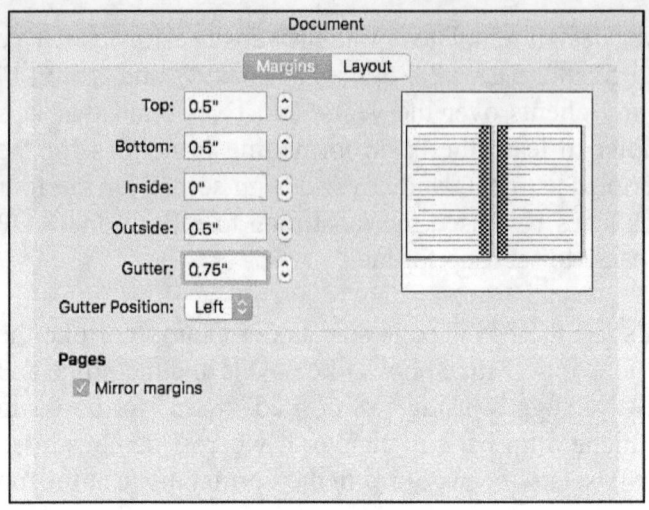

You can see from the preview window on the right side that the space where the pages will go into the spine is colored in, showing that the book pages will open from the middle. Since the mirrored margin's option is checked, every odd numbered page (starting at page one with the first right hand page) will have an inside margin of 0 but a gutter of .75" so the text will not be cut off when the spine is bound.

> **Note**: The print-on-demand portion of KDP used to be separate as "CreateSpace," switching to one process and company in late 2018. The following formatting information is from CreateSpace, but it applies to how you need to learn to set up the format of the book.

I learned to do this formatting correctly by searching around on CreateSpace's members' community forums until I found this article: https://bit.ly/2m4YDUv. From there, I messed around with different page sizes and worked with various print books (ordering hardcopy proofs where necessary) and verifying format on the online-proofing software to make sure I had it right. As I've said before, freelancing is a much about knowing how to find and learn the information you need as it is about being a grammar genius.

> **Reminder**! Select "Whole Document" in the "Apply To" box at the bottom of the window, and turn Track Changes off to make major changes like document size and margins. Also, at the publishing stage, you should be working with a completely edited document and Track Changes should be off with all changes accepted.

> **Formatting Tip**: Unsure what line spacing to apply to the document? Look at other printed books in the book's genre. What line spacing do they use? Some genres use 1.0 (Single) spacing, while others seem to use mostly 1.5 or 2.0 spacing. Then, consider what readers in the genre might prefer. Hopefully you're editing in your niche and know what you as a reader prefer to see in a book format in your genre. I went with single spacing in this book but with hard returns between each paragraph because I wanted to make sure it was easy to read and didn't look too text-heavy on each page. My goal was to allow the format to aid you in absorbing the information I'm giving you and fortify your editing skills. You shouldn't have to squint or give yourself a headache reading my tutorials.

When you have your document formatted and are ready to get it on KDP to publish, you'll need to generate a PDF of the Word document. There are two ways to do this. First, you can go to "save as" under "File" and click "export to PDF." If you get an error message that the text will be "outside of the printable area," you will need to re-define the printable area in the document.

To adjust the non-printable area, go to File, Page Setup, select the "Paper Size" dropdown box and select "Manage Custom Sizes." Select "User Defined Area" under the Non-Printable Area section and change all the values to 0.

The second way to generate your PDF is to go to File, Print, and at the bottom-left corner select the drop-down box. Then, click "Save as PDF."

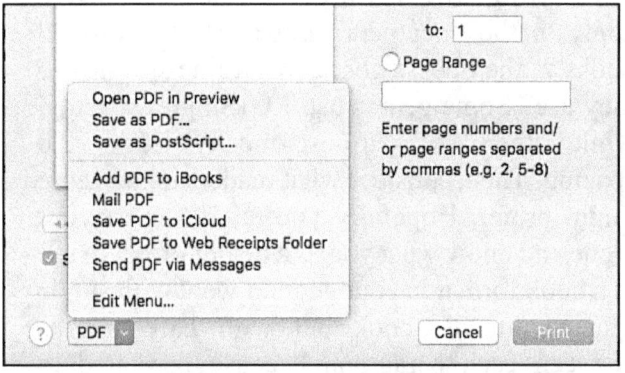

I prefer to use this second way to generate my document PDFs. In the popup window, choose your document title, author name, and save title.

Your complete interior document PDF is the document you need to upload to CreateSpace.

*Cover Design Basics*

We'll go into specific details of cover design in chapter 8, but I want to give you the basic formula you'll need to determine cover design document size.

You know your interior document size already. Let's stick with our 5x8 page size example. For the cover design PDF for KDP, you need to have back cover+spine+front cover in one complete picture/design. KDP suggests adding a .125" bleed to the edges of the design where you don't put any words or key pieces of design. The "bleed" is the safety net. So the width of our cover design without the spine width would be .125+5+5+.125=10.25". Calculating the spine width is slightly more complicated. Get ready for math...*cringe*.

CreateSpace gave the necessary equation on their page titled, "How to Create a Cover for your Book":
- For cream colored pages, multiply page count by .0025
- For white colored pages, multiply page count by .002252
- For colored pages multiply page count by .002347

In our example, let's say we have a 223-page book and we want white pages: 223x.002252= 0.5" (rounded). Add that to the page width. The calculation in order of appearance on your screen, then is .125+5+0.5+5+.125=10.75". The total width of your cover design is 10.75". We'll get into the specifics of setting up and creating your cover designs using these formulas and information in chapter 8.

*KDP Account*

When I help an author self-publish with CreateSpace, I set up their account (using a generic password they can change when we are done publishing their book) so that I can make sure all of the processes go smoothly through to publication. I suggest you learn what KDP publishing accounts offer. When you sign up (using an author's email and other basic information), you'll be instructed to create a new project.

You'll input the title information (author, language, etc.) and the ISBN number and then upload your documents.

**A note on the ISBN number**: Talk to your authors about how much control they want to have over their book. If they want a free ISBN number through KDP, that's fine, but that means they cannot take their book to any other platforms and KDP will show up as their "publisher." Authors can purchase their own, independent ISBN number through sellers like Bowker and can then list their own publisher name. One ISBN number is $125, or an author can purchase 10 ISBN numbers for $295. Expensive, I know, but it is well worth the freedom and control, in my opinion.

After you upload your documents in the Review section, you'll submit your files for free review. You can then view the book in an online proofing software, and/or you and your author can purchase print proofs for review. For your first book project through KDP, I suggest you get a printed proof (and charge it to your author). If you see any errors, you can edit, re-upload, and resubmit your files for review. I've had cover design errors show up on KDP that I didn't catch until I saw the printed proof. Your job is to make sure there aren't any errors in formatting or cover design, so be thorough in this process.

> **Note on Uploading Documents**: KDP may flag your document if you don't imbed your font in the document. If you use common fonts, such as Times New Roman, it isn't a requirement that you imbed the font. Also, while cover art font can be a less common font without issue, using uncommon fonts in the interior document can give you printing issues. I recommend using only common fonts for your interior text. Also, if the interior document includes photos, make sure the photos are at 300dpi or higher quality. The online proof will flag the photos regardless of the dpi level to note that they may appear flattened in printing. Get a print copy proof if you're concerned about the appearance of the photos.

The distribution tab is where you'll decide on the price of the book and in which sales channels your print edition will be available. You'll also pick the cover finish (glossy or matte options are available) and write the book description.

*Tax Info*
One final note on using KDP: your author will need to input his or her tax information in order to publish the book and receive royalty payments. You'll see a note in the project dashboard when you need to direct your author to the input section. Ask your author to sign into the account and input the tax information. Remember this information must remain strictly confidential and

assure your client that you will not access the information on the account at any time.

Now that you know the basics of publishing for print-on-demand, let's talk about eBook publishing.

# 7

## eBooks

Raise your hand if you've read or seen an eBook in the last week. Yeah, all of you. EBooks are all over the world of publishing, and as an editor, you need to know how to create them.

The eBook movement is new to a lot of authors in older (and parts of the younger) generations, and they will look to their editors to guide them through the publishing process in this newer format.

I say a lot that I like working with new editors the most. While I appreciate the incredible learning experience that comes from working with more established authors, I find I have the greatest connection to newbie authors. Newbie authors know they have a story to share, they know they want to self-publish (because even though they don't know how to self-publish, it is much less terrifying than attempting to learn how to get in on traditional publishing), and they know they need help to accomplish their publishing goal.

I explain this very straight forward thing to new authors: If you don't have an eBook version of your book, you won't sell enough books to cover your production costs.

Why do you need to know how to format, design, and publish eBooks for Kindle? Simple: Kindle is the platform with the most customers and the most straightforward eBook publishing process. Much of what I already covered in chapter 4 will come into play in the eBook formatting process, so look there for reference when needed.

*Document format*
I already explained how to create mirrored margins in your print book so you can ensure no text will be cut off when the spine was bound. For Kindle, you don't need to format with mirrored margins. In fact, you don't necessarily have to use a specific page size for Kindle.

If your book consists entirely of text—meaning the design beyond chapter breaks is irrelevant—you can simply add the other necessary elements to a generic file format that contains the text of the book and upload it to Kindle.

*Live TOCs*
The first major difference between print and eBooks is the importance of a live Table of Contents in eBooks for Kindle. Amazon Kindle has searchable and clickable link capabilities, and with a live TOC, the eBook you put together can automatically have clickable links for readers to easily navigate between parts of the book. Here's how to create one.

The first step in creating a live TOC is to assign heading styles to your chapter titles and any sections that need to be listed in the TOC. Go back to the heading styles section in chapter 4 for instruction on how to assign styles to text.

Then, after you've given a heading style to all the necessary sections, go to a page where you want to put the TOC and find the Table of Contents icon in the References tab:

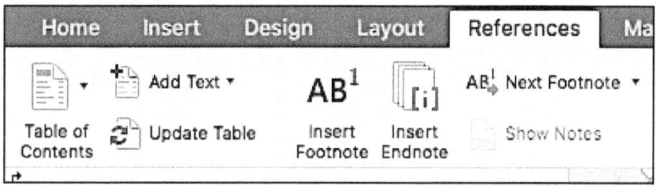

In the dropdown box, find a style you like and select it—or create your own if you're so inclined. The page you are on in the document will automatically populate with the text you defined with Header 1, 2, or 3 styles (or the styles you created yourself). If you used more than one header style (perhaps using Header 1 for chapter titles and Header 2 for sections in the chapter), the text will show up in different levels on the TOC.

**Tips**:
1. Again, if you want to change the font of your TOC after you create it, click and hold in the line above or below the start or end of the table and highlight the text.
2. It is good practice to update the page numbers at the end of the editing process, but the page numbers won't actually show up in the TOC in the Kindle eBook. The headers will show up as clickable links and when a reader clicks the link, the eBook will jump to that chapter/heading.

*Kindle Direct Publishing Platform*

Here is a tip from the Amazon Kindle Direct platform support team:

> The initial formatting you've chosen in Word may be altered slightly to conform to Kindle device specifications. For optimum readability on the Kindle device, it is best to save your Word (DOC / DOCX) file as "Web Page - filtered" or "HTML - filtered." Don't upload your content with Track Changes on...Review your content in Word after you've saved it as HTML and make any necessary changes, saving it again. Then upload the HTML file in Amazon KDP.

You will need to save the document as a Web Page, Filtered document. Go to save as and select this option:

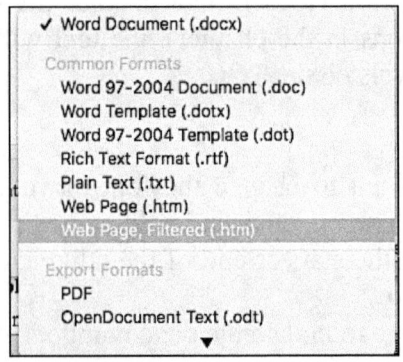

If your document contains any images, the images will be saved into a folder in the same place where you saved your .htm document of the interior text. To ensure your images show up large enough to view on a kindle reader, use 8.5x11 page size for your entire document and make images as large as possible in the document before saving it as an .htm.

Then, when you go to upload your document to the eBook section of KDP, you need to "zip" the .htm document and the images folder together to upload. Click to select one, then hold "Shift" to select the other. Then right click and select "Compress 2 items."

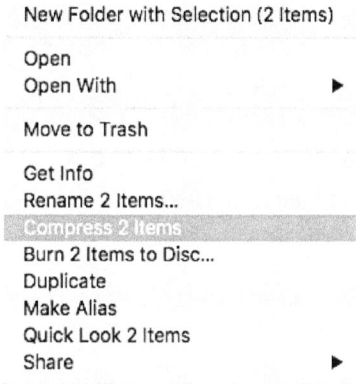

A zipped file will appear. Rename it the title of the book and "for eBook." The zip file is what you will upload on KDP.

Your cover design will automatically transfer from the print-on-demand version of the book, but if for some reason it doesn't, make sure you save the front cover only (not the spine and back cover content) as a .jpg file to upload on KDP. More on that in the next chapter.

**Other eBook formatting tips**:
1. Remove the headers/footers text from the document—including page numbers—before you save the document as an .htm and upload the zip files to KDP. The pages will be different for Kindle than for print anyway, so the page

numbers and headers are insignificant in the eBook.
2. If the font is vital to the design of the book you're working on, make sure you embed your fonts before you upload your document.
3. If you're publishing a children's book or graphic novel, see the KDP discussion boards or "help" section for specific details on how to accomplish that. Life-long learner mode: activate!

Now let's talk about designing an eye-catching cover for your clients' books.

# 8

## Cover Design on Canva.com

Until fall of 2016, I thought the best, or really the only, way to create a decent cover design was by learning the super complex Adobe InDesign software. I worked myself through the basics of InDesign to create some decent cover designs for my clients, and I paid over $30 a month to have the software on my computer through the Adobe Creative Cloud. But when one of my colleagues asked if I'd heard of Canva, my design services changed drastically for the better.

Canva is a free online design kit. You can create everything from a Facebook header to a beautiful slideshow presentation to a fancy resume on Canva. With free photos and graphics, plenty of fonts, sizes, and colors, and all the document sizes you could ever need, Canva is a great online software for creating cover designs.

While you can use Canva for free, there are a lot of benefits to purchasing the yearly Canva for business subscription. The paid version allows you to upload and store a logo, brand colors, and brand fonts. The paid version is useful for building your brand for your editing business. If you're hesitant to purchase the membership for business, start clicking around on the free version until you get the hang of it. But where InDesign can cost upwards of $350 per year, the paid account on Canva is only $160. I'm all about saving all the moneys.

The screenshots below are from my paid account, so your free version will look slightly different. Sign up with Facebook or an email address and let's create a cover for a make-believe novel (was that overly descriptive?).

*Basic Setup*
Now is the time again when we have to use a little bit of every humanities student's least favorite thing...*math*. Ew. Go back and use the formulas I gave you to determine the width of your document, with the spine size and bleed area included. Also, add .125" of bleed area to the top and bottom of the document to determine the height of the document. Using the same example I set up earlier, our document in Canva will need to be 10.75"x8.25".

Before you start mocking up a cover design, do a little research. Let's say the genre of the book we're creating a cover design for is fantasy fiction. Go on Amazon and type in "Fantasy Fiction."

Make notes on various elements the cover designs you see that work well for other fantasy novels. I see mostly computer graphics of fantastical animals (like dragons) or dark castles. There are a lot of dark sky scenes or metallic colors. I also see covers with one focal point—a character or object.

Now that you have an idea of the kinds of designs other books in the genre use—which clearly work well for selling books in the genre—it's time to set up your document and start working on some ideas.

In your Canva account, go to "Create a Design" and select "Use Custom Dimensions." Create a 10.75" x 8.25" document.

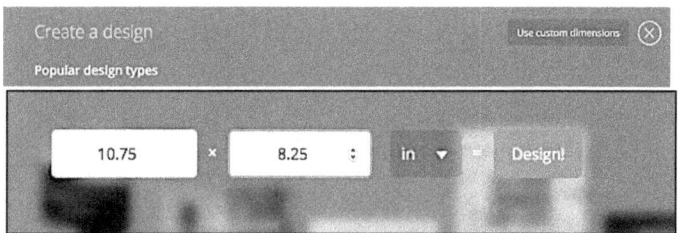

**Note**: If you use the business account you have the option to change the dimensions of your document at any time. If you stick with the free account, you must set your dimensions at the beginning and you won't be able to change them after you create the blank document.

Then you can start designing your cover. Here is an example for a fantasy fiction book I edited and published:

As you can see, the cover design is set up "back cover-spine-front cover." The white block on the back cover is where KDP will put the bar code for the book when it is printed. You'll want to delete that white box before you upload it to KDP, but put it in as you're designing so you make sure the bar code won't cover anything important. Canva is really easy to use. Just start clicking around on there, and before you know it, you'll have a cover design and a new hobby. When you're done, simply download it as a PDF and upload the PDF on KDP.

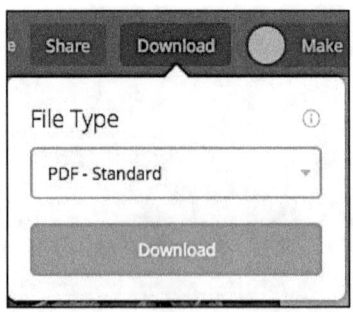

Canva offers endless options for designing cover art for books. Here are some screen shots of what Canva has to offer in the design tabs:

There are free and paid photos, tons of font choices, pre-made designs and layouts, a place to upload your logos, photos, and other designs, icons, shapes, and anything else you could imagine to add or use in your cover design.

*Photos and Graphics*
You may be able to find a free photo on Canva to use on your cover design, but I prefer to search pixabay.com for attribution-free photos.

Pixabay is free. Download as high a quality photo as possible so you are sure to have the best possible resolution when your cover design is printed.

If you find a photo on Creative Commons or another website that specifies attributions and photo licenses, make sure you make note of those details and include them in your cover design. If I use a photo that requires attribution, I put that information to the left of the bar code on the back cover (i.e., *cover photo by*:). I also include the attribution and license information on the copyright page.

You can also use Adobe InDesign to create cover designs, though the software is much more advanced. There are dozens of InDesign classes you can take online, so I won't go into specifics of design with InDesign here. Use the Google-box, y'all. It has all the answers to your InDesign software questions.

> **Design Tip**: The eye tends to see "center" as slightly above and right of center. Keep that in mind when you design your cover. If you want an element in a photo or text to look "centered," move it a few clicks above and to the right of the dead center line.

Time to switch gears a little and discuss the business side of this, well, business.

# Part 2: Business-ey Things

# 9

## Business Formation & Money Talk

Though I've been in business for a little over five years, I am still not business brained. I don't understand much about taxes or business structure (though I've tried to at least have a working knowledge of both for my own sake), and what I do understand I have a hard time explaining to other people. I go to a CPA for my tax filing needs and I use a super-low key business structure called a sole proprietorship that even I can follow. I count on my friends and colleagues to come to the rescue when I have "businessey" questions, and one of those folks was kind enough to write this chapter for me (and you!) about business formation for freelancers like us. Take it away, Chris!

### Business Formation for Freelancers
By Christopher Draper

I set up my first company in 2002 when I was very much in your shoes: only a year out of college, ready to make a killing at this whole "business" thing, and eyeballs deep in a labyrinth of help documents and business advice blogs. Between LLCs, LP, LLPs, LLTs, B-Corps, C-Corps, PBJ-Corps, and S-Corps (some of which aren't even real…just testing you!) located in Delaware, the Caymans, Wyoming, Pittsburgh, or Sydney, it is nearly impossible to break down what is important and what is just noise. This section is not designed to answer all of the questions that someone going into business should ask. Rather, it is intended to help you get into the right ballpark and figure your way through from there as the eternal learners you all are.

When dealing with business formation, there are a few things to remember:

1. Your business type only matters if you make money.
2. Your taxes will always be less than what you're paid, so worry about getting paid first.
3. There is no wrong answer; nearly everything is correctable.

Why so many options?

The reason there are so many help blogs on business formation is because there are so many different things people can tweak and optimize when it comes to business structure and operations. If you're running some large, international, tax advantaged business that ships unknown items between a bunch of random people, you need to be in the weeds...

But you're a writer or editor. Your business is to write and edit. Your business is not to be in the business of being a business.

For young people or companies that are just starting out, picking a business structure comes down to three simple questions:

1. Will you pay yourself most of the money you make from one or more clients?
2. Will you work with contractors or make any large purchases?
3. Will you be doing something with a bunch of other partners or so risky (e.g., launching a network of white supremacist ghostwriters) that your business has a real chance of landing in court?

If you can answer "YES, THAT'S ME" to either numbers two or three, forming an LLC or some form of a Corporation would be important to you.

*I need a company!*
Without creating a Limited Liability Corporation (LLC), a Corporation (C-Corp), or one of its derivatives, you cannot buy healthcare or open a business bank account.

While we all need healthcare, just because a business buys it does not make it cheaper. You still need to be making good money to get good healthcare, and going through a business to buy it may prevent you from getting many of the subsidies that exist if you are just getting started making an income. While there are tax advantages and all the rest to forming a company that can buy your healthcare, if you are forming a business to secure healthcare through a Professional Employment Organization (which I HIGHLY recommend) or directly from an insurance company, your business acumen may be a bit more advanced than this section is designed to support.

Regarding banking, you will often need a business bank account if you are paying contractors, receiving funds from a large number of clients, or making large purchases. In addition to it being good business practice to silo all of your business transactions in a separate account, business bank accounts will also give you access to a much wider range of financial products from your bank. However, most of these products will almost always be backed by your personal finances when you're small, so while you can theoretically use them, the reality is that you're in the same boat you were in before you formed your company (sorry to get your hopes up there…).

*So which company type do I pick?*
Now if you know you need a company (FYI, this is probably not you if you are reading this book right now, so I'll try to make this as meaningfully brief as I can…), the next question is whether you want it to be a pass-through taxation entity. If your business is a pass-through entity (i.e., LLC, S-Corp, etc.), it means your business is tied to your personal taxes. The money you make counts as part of your *personal taxes*, the deductions you get to take are slightly more advantageous, yet you have to file your taxes every year (even when you don't make money) at a cost that is often more expensive than doing just your personal returns. If you are buying expensive computers, vehicles, or other business items that are "deductible" (meaning you get to reduce the amount of money you earn by the cost of these items), an LLC may make some sense.

If you are in a more risky business, have a bunch of partners that may come in or out of the business, or may not make money for a while, a traditional Corporation is probably better and cheaper for you to form and manage. For small companies of only a few people, C-Corps are usually cheaper to set up, you can end your tax year any time so you can pick a time of year when accountants are cheaper, oversight in most states is very reasonable, and failed businesses just go away. You aren't stuck filing expensive versions of your personal taxes for years and years.

Unless you have a lot of property or expenses running through your company, a C-Corp is better for people who need a company that could potentially fail. As a warning, this is counter to the advice a lawyer or accountant will often tell you. The cynic in me would point out that lawyers and accountants make more money off of a small LLC than a small C-Corp. But as a realist, this is the normal recommendation simply because most people normally recommend it. That's it. But if you find yourself if in a lawyer's office and they are recommending an LLC, ask them: "I'm a small business that has no idea what I will become, no idea who my partners may be some day, and it could easily fail. Why is an LLC better for me?" and see what they say.

But the real point: you probably don't need to worry about any of that in order to get started.

*What's really important to get started*
If you are contracted to do specific tasks on your own for individuals or companies that you know both exist and are above board, don't worry about jumping head first into forming a specific kind of business. Operate as yourself, file your taxes with TurboTax, and identify your income on Schedule C for contract work. You will still be able to deduct expenses (just like in an LLC), so keep your receipts, but you won't have the hassle of managing a complex business that takes your focus away from your business:

Getting people to pay you to write and edit.

\*\*

Thanks, Chris!

## Money Talk

One other topic we should touch on in this section is how you'll actually get paid and the money set-up you might need for tax purposes. Here's what I do for The Writing Mechanic.

*PayPal*
I have a PayPal account linked to my business account at my bank. I send out PayPal invoices to clients who choose to pay that way. Then, when they pay the invoice, the money goes into my PayPal wallet and I can transfer it into my business account.

*Personal Checks*
I definitely prefer to get personal checks because then I don't have to pay the PayPal fees. I ask clients to mail me checks, or, if I'm local, I swing by and pick them up.

*Bank Account for The Writing Mechanic*
I have a small business bank account for The Writing Mechanic. I simply requested an EIN (Employer Identification Number) or TIN (Tax Identification Number) from the government online and used that as I would my own social security number to open the account at my chosen institution. I chose a small bank because there was no minimum balance and no fees for my little business. I run the money from my projects through that account and then pay myself out of the

business account by writing myself a check out of my business account and depositing that check into my personal account.

*Contracts & Deposits*
If you're working with a new client, consider establishing a contract that dictates how much you will be paid to complete the work. That way, if you had a client skip town with your work, you could bring the contract to court and get your money. I've never had that issue, and I don't generally work with contracts, but I know many editors who don't work without one because they've had truly awful experiences.

What I do instead is work on a deposit system. I do a sample edit for the client, they can see my work, and I ask for a deposit (usually around $300-400 depending on the size of the project). I then begin work and send them a partially completed section of the book equaling that deposit amount part way through the process. Then, I complete the project, send them the final invoice, and when they pay the invoice, I send them the completed project. The system works well for me and my clients seem to like it.

*What I Keep Track of for Taxes (What I Send my CPA in March Every Year)*
I keep track of every dollar I make for editing projects. If you're working with individual authors, they probably won't have you fill out a w9 tax form, but you still need to keep track of what they pay you and claim that income on your yearly taxes. Companies and publishing entities will likely ask you to fill out that w9 and will send you a w2 form at the end of the year that shows how much they paid you. I give all of that information to my CPA.

I also keep track of what I pay for operations costs each year, including internet services, website costs, EFA membership costs, etc. Anything I have to pay for that is necessary for me to do my job, I keep track of. That is all deductible in taxes. In my state, I can even deduct a percentage of my monthly rent based on the size of my designated home office. Another thing to keep track of is any traveling you do to meet with clients. Keep track of your mileage and any expenses you incur throughout the year to meet with potential or current clients.

It's also a good practice to pay quarterly taxes throughout the year. My CPA gave me an estimate of what I should pay quarterly based on what I made the year prior, so I can just send in that amount every quarter. That helps me avoid having to pay a huge sum of income tax at the end of the year. Obviously, you'll need to wait until you've worked for a year to know how much you could potentially need to pay quarterly, but it's never too early to find a solid CPA.

OK. Enough business-ey stuff. Let's get back to something I think is more fun: your online presence!

# 10

## Get Online

I know we Millennials don't *need* another excuse to be on the internet, but building your own business website can be a fantastic way to learn a little web design, grow your network, and bring more clients into the fold. What should your editing services website be? What should it include?

Could, should, would—it's all relative. I can speak only from my own experience. I'm not a pro web designer, and I'm most definitely not a coder, but I've figured the ins and outs of a basic, functioning WordPress website and a far simpler SquareSpace website page for The Writing Mechanic, and it has served me well thus far.

A quick note here: When I first started my business, I thought the majority of my clients would find me on my website through Google or another search engine. I spent a lot of money and time creating a website, but what I've noticed over the last few years is that while it is good to have at least a webpage about your editing services (and YOU as a person) available for people to look at, 99.9% of my clients have found me in other ways. We'll talk about those different places where clients have found me in the next few chapters. So take it from my experience: keep your website simple. If you want to blog for fun, like I do on my website kathrinherr.com, just include your business page as a piece of your website. Link to that page on your social media profiles so people can find you in those other places and then visit your page to learn a little more. Or use SquareSpace to create a couple of pages where you can send your potential clients.

*Business Name*
I chose my business name based on the type of editing I wanted to provide. My favorite types of editing are developmental and copy, so I thought about those types as I came up with possible names. I chose The Writing Mechanic as a clever play on the mechanics of writing (or "the writing mechanics") because I edit manuscripts so that they adhere to good mechanics. I fix what's broke in the manuscript (before you freak out, that was intentionally poor grammar...), so I'm The Writing Mechanic.

I've helped other editors come up with names for their editing businesses, but every name is entirely dependent on the editor's style, services, and personality. One name I suggested was the Moody Manuscript Mender (all for alliteration!). My colleague Ethan Zierke founded EZ Editing (get it? How clever, E...Z.). One of my other colleagues' businesses is called Write From the Inside Out. She is a memoir editor and writing workshop leader, so that name fits perfectly. Whatever name you choose, make sure it says something about the services you provide and maybe a little about you as a person.

Your business name is part of your brand as a business, and the brand you're selling is the YOU brand. We'll discuss the importance of being authentically you in everything you post on social media in the next chapter, but consider how you want to package up your skills, experience, and personality into a marketable brand for your company. You might even benefit from doing a brand workshop or class or filling out a brand workbook. My favorite business guide extraordinaire is Wonderlass, Allison Marshall. See the appendices for links to her awesomeness.

## Websites

When you go to create your website, then, look for a domain name that is either your business name or your name. Authors are encouraged to use their name as their website name so that they will be searchable by name rather than book title, since many authors want to write more than one book in their careers. If you want to write and sell books as part of your business, or if you happen to have a large social media following based on your personal "name brand," consider using your own name for the domain. Otherwise, there is a good chance your potential clients will search for something like "editing services" and will more likely click on a domain with a business name as opposed to a personal name. If you choose the business name route, create a stellar "About Me" page to tell your story and humanize yourself to your readers and potential clients.

After you decide on your domain name (and make sure it is available by checking GoDaddy or another domain market), you'll need to decide where you want to host your website before purchasing the domain. I used to use WordPress, but that is just one of the website platforms you could choose. Then, some hosting services for WordPress (such as Bluehost) include a domain host in their platform. Others, such as WP Engine—my former host of choice—does not include a domain name market, so you'll have to purchase the domain through GoDaddy or something like it. Other website types, like SquareSpace, have all-in-one hosting and domain packages. The hosting package will probably be the most expensive part of your website build, but you probably can't build an editing empire without one, so open that wallet, yo. Just make sure you do some research (and get on with some live chats with sales people) to find the best hosting option for you.

I previously hosted my website through Bluehost, but when I purchased my website, Google did not require websites to have an SSL (Secure Site Lock) certificate in order to rank high in search-engine results. When Google changed their requirements, I tried to add an SSL to my website but it effectively shut it down for 24 hours (to which I responded with a meltdown of my own). So, I went searching for a hosting platform that would include an SSL certificate and wouldn't shut down my website. I found WP Engine to have the best customer service and technical support, so I jumped over to them. The transfer was painful. I suggest you go with WP Engine first if you choose WordPress for your editing services website and avoid the hassle, or another hosting platform if another better suits your fancy. (When I switched to WP Engine, I also transferred my domain name to GoDaddy. That wasn't *nearly* as much of a hassle as switching the host...)

But once I got everything successfully transferred and worked out every kink (a long process that taught me a ton about website design and only made me pull about half of my hair out), my WordPress site could just sit comfortably online as the place where I send potential clients.

Here was the basic setup of my website when I was on WordPress website:
1. I purchased a theme ($59) in the MoJo Marketplace on my WordPress website that allowed me to create individual pages and also include a separate blog and blog categories. I chose The Core theme for my website and used a child theme. I then set up my website pages, my shop, and my blog in the theme.
2. I created these sections: Home, About Me (with a contact form), Shop, and Blog. WordPress uses plugins for things like your services shop.
3. I had already written a number of blog posts, so I re-uploaded each blog post and created categories for subjects in my blog: Writing Tips, NP Correspondence (one of my personal projects), and Client Interviews.
4. I installed and activated a bunch of plugins that allowed me to sell products, receive donations, create forum discussions for my clients, and improve my SEO.

Here's the truth, folks. I had written about four pages worth of content about how I used WordPress. I wrote about all of the plug-ins I used and all of the pieces I had in place before I made the switch to SquareSpace. But I don't think a WordPress website with a "shop" is the best way for a freelance editor to go anymore. I tried it all that way and it didn't work for me.

Nowadays, I think it's best to simply use your online presence through your website as a place for potential clients to learn more about you, your experience, and your services. Until you get incredibly busy with editing projects, you will be able to handle invoicing on your own. You probably won't need an online shop to handle the invoices for you automatically. When you get to the point that it's more work than you want to do because you're busy editing, consider purchasing an invoicing software or hiring someone to handle the invoicing process for you. But, y'all, I've been doing this for almost eight years and I still send out my invoices myself. I don't need a shop to sell my editing services anymore. I like controlling when my invoices go out and how I send them. It's an important part of closing out my projects. My webpage serves instead as a "get to know Kathrin" page. I link to it from my LinkedIn Profile and my EFA profile and people who are already interested in my services from finding me on those channels visit my website to get to know me a little better. The sales themselves don't come from the website. The actual sales of my services come from my personal communication with each of my clients.

**SquareSpace**
The website platform I recommend is SquareSpace. You can see my website kathrinherr.com for an example of a SquareSpace website. That is where I have my webpage for The Writing Mechanic. I just have a simple page where I highlight some of my favorite editing projects and talk about myself and my services. Also, go to GreatSexChristianStyle.com to see an example of an author website I created for a client using SquareSpace. SquareSpace is *wayyyy* easier to use than WordPress. It is a visual builder and is entirely optimized for non-

coders like me. SquareSpace is where my current website now lives...and we are oh-so-happy there.

If you plan use your website as more of an online portfolio and blog, SquareSpace may be right for you. I set up a beautiful SquareSpace website in only a weekend...I've heard you should be able to do that with WordPress too, but it took me more like four months to get everything working correctly on WordPress. The SquareSpace package is also less expensive for small businesses than WordPress.

If you decide to use SquareSpace as your website provider, here are the pages and sections you may want to create:
- A stellar home page showcasing recent blog posts, info about you, your services and rates, and your experience, and any other relevant info your clients might want to see right off the bat
- A blog (or multiple blogs if you want categories that show up in your navigation! Check out KathrinHerr.com to see what I mean)
- An "About Me" page with a fun biographical note and info about your experience—maybe even your resume and links to your social media accounts where your clients and potential clients can follow you
- A reviews section where you post testimonials from your clients

Some editors do the website thing extremely well. Check out Editor Megan Harris' website (and Facebook Page!) for one awesome example: http://mharriseditor.com/.

Again, I trimmed everything down to only have a one-page "summary" for The Writing Mechanic. We'll talk a little about this in the next two chapters, but when I learned that my clients—my ideal clients—were finding me on the EFA and on LinkedIn and only visiting my webpage to get to know me a little bit before sending me an email to inquire about my services, I realized how unnecessary a full website was for my particular editing business. Instead, I get to use kathrinherr.com as my hub for all of the parts of my business and building an online community of readers while also using it as a place where potential clients can see some about me and my business.

> **Reminder**! It baffles me that I might have to say this, but if I don't I fear that someone will fail in this area (and blame me for it...). So here it goes: EDIT THE TEXT ON YOUR EDITING WEBSITE/WEBPAGE. MAKE SURE YOU DON'T HAVE ANY ERRORS. I know, DUH, but you know as well as I do that someone won't remember that part and will come off looking like a total newbie hypocrite. Don't be that guy, Carl. Present a professional website or webpage with edited text so you look like the kind of professional who should be editing books. Deal? Good. Glad we got that out of the way.

Now let's talk about where many of your clients will start to find you: Social Media.

# 11

## Social Media

Along with your general web presence through your website or webpage, social media is a good way to help build your online visibility and begin the process of building trust with potential clients. I assume most of you are well acquainted with at least one social media platform and that you will be able to figure out other platforms quickly. Here are the platforms I'm on and how I use them as a freelance editor.

*LinkedIn*
The platform that has given me the most return on time investment in my editing business is LinkedIn. LinkedIn is a professional network. You can fill out your profile and have it act as your extended resume. You can join groups, post blogs, and engage in conversations with other professionals.

But to be honest, I don't do much connecting on LinkedIn at all. I filled out my profile with a lot of detail (paying special attention to my professional title and description), linked it to my webpage and other online profiles, added my email address, and let it stand. I update it every few months.

Just make sure you keep your profile up to date even if you don't do much on the platform. I had one of my biggest client connections come from someone looking on LinkedIn for an editor with my experience located in my area of the country. If I had been completely lax with my profile, Ashley never would have found me and looked to see what I was all about! Thanks to my LinkedIn profile, I now have an editing services connection that has produced multiple projects in only a few months.

Whatever editing services you want to offer (refer back to chapter 2 if you need help figuring that out), make sure you name them in your title/description so your potential clients can find you based on the work they need you for.

*Facebook*
Facebook this is the platform I use the least for promoting my editing business. Facebook has really been most useful for me in connecting with current and former clients. I've befriended a lot of my clients on Facebook and I like to keep up with what they're doing in general aside from the books we are publishing together. Many of my clients have been repeat customers, and by staying connected with them "personally" on Facebook, they always think of me first when they have a new project. They also will send their friends to me, and they can do so easily when we're friends on Facebook. It's also fun to be able to shoot one of them an email when I see something they did on Facebook (like Ned who ran a marathon). It's really great to be able to connect on a deeper level with my authors through the Facebook platform.

Some editors and authors really thrive on Facebook. I know some even pay a lot for advertising on Facebook. I tried that for a month...it was a waste of money in my case. But that is just my experience! Check out editors like Megan Harris for a really good Facebook example.

You might find that Facebook is where your clients find you, and if so, AWESOME. I think it depends a lot on your niche and the kinds of services you offer. If you're a proofreading genius and a style-guide editor, you might have great luck getting clients through Facebook. Since I focus more on my ghostwriting, developmental editing, copyediting, and self-publishing services, I need to connect in a more professional way upfront (to convince authors of my skills and experience) and then use email communication and sample edits to gain authors as clients. The social media connection comes after I've gained their trust as a client. Your experience might be different.

*Instagram*
Like Facebook, I use Instagram as a platform to help potential clients learn more about me. Your main goal on all social media is to *build trust*. Authors are people, in case you didn't know, and people want to work with people they can relate to and trust. Instagram is a fun tool to give your network an insight into your life beyond the red pen.

Can you keep a secret? I thought so... Here it goes. Truth bomb: I don't have it all together. I often wish I had a giant red pen of life that I could use to correct all of my mistakes and shortcomings. And I'm not just talking about my business. Every aspect of my life could use a little red pen action.

But when I am real with all of that on my social media, people relate to my shortcomings and my fears and are more likely to see me as a person rather than just a ruthless red-pen-wielder.

I post about my running plan when I train for races; I post tons of pictures of my dog; and I post about some of my other interests. My Instagram feed helps paint the full picture of who I am—the lady behind the red pen, The Writing Mechanic and the runner, coffee addict, dog lover, and sustainability seeker.

*Pinterest*
Pinterest is another visual-heavy platform, and while I'm certain it can be used to explode your exposure and grow your network, I find it more conducive to getting my creative juices flowing to expand my content as a writer. Also, if you decide to start a blog, Pinterest can be a MAJOR page-view catalyst for you.

Pinterest isn't really a social media platform. It is a search engine! You can use is to increase your own knowledge base, get ideas for your own projects, and connect with other people who are doing the things you are doing or are wanting to do. And if you post your own blogs to Pinterest, they become more searchable and can increase your exposure.

Like Facebook, you can run ads on Pinterest. I personally have not paid for Pinterest advertising before, but the process looks simpler than it is on Facebook with fewer elements to take into account. Jenna Kutcher has an amazing podcast and she talks about using Pinterest. She makes it simple. You'll find her in the appendices.

*Twitter*

Ok, now we're way out of my comfort zone. I'm only 27 years old, but somehow I missed the Twitter wave and I haven't been able to catch it yet. 140 characters—while potentially a fun, poetic way of writing—and posting hundreds of times a day are just not the way I think. I don't get it.

BUT that doesn't mean you shouldn't use Twitter for your business! So many established authors and publications hang out on Twitter. Editors galore. Twitter can be an amazing place to engage with your potential clients and grow you network. If you're a haiku-writing quick talker, Twitter might be the perfect social media platform for you.

As you're probably able to see from all of this, I think it's a good idea to have a presence on all of the different platforms in general (that you're ultra-visible online) so that your potential clients can get to know you through all channels. You're trying to build trust, remember. So what I recommend is that you set up all the basics on the various platforms or just adjust your personal accounts (I know you all have them) so that you put your services out there for people to see. You never know whose mom's pastor's wife's friend will need an editor, and if you're on Facebook and you talk every once in a while about your editing business (don't overwhelm people with salesy ads, though) your mom might tell her pastor who will tell his wife who will tell her friend and you'll have an editing gig. (Yes, that exact thing happened to me, and I got to work with an awesome lady on her family genealogy project!)

*Scheduling Posts: Convenience*
If you want to really go for it and build your network like crazy on social media, you might want to consider scheduling your posts. You aren't going to be paid for the time you spend on social media. You're a one-person show. You are simultaneously the CEO, secretary, marketing expert, and accountant. You can't spend hours a day growing your social media following when you're first starting out in this business.

Consider scheduling your posts on your various accounts using tools like Hootsuite and Tailwind. If you spend just an hour a week scheduling your posts (plus 15 minutes a day responding to comments and engaging with your network), you'll save time and be able to do things you'll actually be paid for.

My favorite scheduling tool is Hootsuite. You can schedule up to three different accounts on the free Hootsuite account, and unless you find more than three platforms that work well for growing your business, I wouldn't recommend paying for an account.

*Best Practices*
There are some basic best practices you should do your best to follow on every social media platform. Here are my top tips for growing your network and visibility online:

**Know why you do what you do so you can share it with your clients in *everything* you post on social media**. Define your vision and mission statements for your company at the start and use them to decide what to post on social media. Keep your message as consistent as possible so your audience understands who you are and what you offer. Consistency in message builds trust, which is—*again*—the whole point of being on social media as a freelancer.

**Be yourself**. Ready for that point again? *Your clients need to trust you*. Build that trust! And build it honestly. Be yourself. Don't try to copy something I'm doing on social media or something any other editor or writer is doing. While I encourage you to *edit* into the voice of your authors, everything you post on social media should be as authentically *you* as possible. Being honest with who you are on social media will not only help your clients trust you enough to want to work with you but will also help keep you consistent in your message, no matter how long you're in this business.

**Be consistent**. Well, you've heard this, what, seven times now? That's how important it is. And I will be the first one to admit that this is not something I've been very good at on social media. I get lazy with my social media posting. But when I'm consistent with my posts and engagement, I can see real growth in my connection to my clients and in how much I *enjoy* being an editor. Being consistent in my message *and* in how and when I post on social media shows my clients that I'm in this field to stay and that I will continue, year after year, to provide value to them. It also gives my clients every reason to refer their friends to me. Plus, when I can connect on a personal level with the *people* behind the words I'm ripping to shreds with my red pen, I truly love my job...so much so that it doesn't even feel like a job anymore.

**Consider writing your business plan *now* and include your social media outline and plan**. Confession time.

My name is Kathrin, and I'm an excessive planner and organizer who lacks follow-through. *("Hi, Kathrin.")* I've been in this business for seven years, and I still don't really have a complete business plan. I have downloaded 50 different templates, half-started half of them, and completely reevaluated my entire business more times than I care to even count. I have the drive to set up my business the "right" way, but my follow-through in that side of things is severely lacking. I can rock the shiz out of client correspondence and follow-through (and I'll share my best tips for such things in the last section of the book), but the business side is ZZZzzzz.... See? I fell asleep writing it.

BUT, I know for certain that if I would just sit down and create my business plan (even a fluid, changeable business plan), my social media strategy and my overall business exposure would be quadruple what it is now.

So maybe do what I say and not what I do...or shoot me an email and we can work on our business plans together. That would be fun! Allison Marshall of Wonderlass.com has a downloadable business plan template that is super simple and is geared toward us creative types. She includes a section on social media planning and marketing too. She's also super fun and has a unicorn onesie that she wears in some of her YouTube videos. Can a person dressed as an animal be a spirit animal? If so, she's mine.

**Create a storyboard!** We're story-lovers, right? So consider creating a social media storyboard for your editing business! Include some personal topics in there too. Write out a storyboard of who you are as a person and a freelancer and how you want people to see you online. Your storyboard could help you decide what to post to attract your ideal clients. Plus, it's FUN! I also have a vision board, and I include dreams and goals I have for every area of my life, including my editing business. I'll talk about that a little more later on.

My biggest tip for using social media to grow your business is to ***utilize social media to connect to your existing network***. Social media is a great way to get connected to people you already know...but do those people know what you do? Do your friends know what kind of work you do? Does your mother? Grandma? Uncle? Cousin? If not, tell them on social media! Share what you do with them. You NEVER know who in your network will know someone who needs your services. Don't bombard your Facebook friends with posts about editing and writing and your services and rates (avoid the "Hey, I'll edit your book for $50/hour" post), but don't stay silent about it either! Make sure people know you're a wordsmith so when their random connection says, "I've been looking for someone to help write/fix/publish my book," they can say, "Oh! You should talk to my daughter/cousin/etc." If they don't know, they can't tell other people about you.

*Resources*
Again, there are hundreds of folks more qualified that I to train you on how to use social media to grow your business exponentially, and I encourage you to seek them out and absorb all the information you can from them.

*Last notes on social media*
I consider social media, like my website, my "online resume" or a "professional 'dating' profile." I have all of my social media platforms filled out so that my prospective clients can find me in all of those places and get to know me. Being present online on social media gives me a way to appeal to my clients and build that ever necessary trust. But even more than social media, other virtual communities have proven vital to my business growth. Let's talk about those.

# 12

## Growing Your Network

In order to get clients, you have to grow your network. Most of my clients have been friends of my colleagues, general social connections, or are from the Editorial Freelancers Association. I spent time growing my network up front, and my business grew—and continues to grow—as a result. While my website and my social media platforms are helpful for building my online presence, the following resources have been more directly linked to my business growth.

*EFA*
The Editorial Freelancers Association is one of my best sources for finding new editing clients. For a yearly membership fee, editors receive project openings via email as authors post them to the EFA website. As a member of the community, I can respond directly to an author if I feel I'm a good fit for the project. I've been hired to work on at least two book projects per year from the EFA, for which I earn more than quadruple my yearly membership fee. With the EFA, potential clients are made available to me and all I have to do is sell my services through sample edits and correspondence. More on that in the next chapter.

But the value of the EFA extends beyond the job posts. Editors living in the same region are often formed into

EFA chapters who meet to discuss the market, participate in a class, or simply network. When I was living in North Carolina, I joined the central North Carolina chapter and met a group of fantastic editors. We discussed the market, drank coffee, and even did a seated yoga class to combat the editor's spine slump. We agreed to refer authors to one another depending on our niche, and it was through a referral from a member of that group that I came to work for Steve and Mary Lowe and edited their book for publication with InterVarsity Press. Since then, Steve and Mary have given my name to their PhD students and colleagues, some of whom have hired me to edit manuscripts that are right in my editing/education sweet spot.

The EFA holds annual conferences, teaches webinars and online classes for editors, and lists its members in an online database that authors can search through. Most recently, a handful of folks have emailed me about working with me because they found my profile on the EFA database. I haven't spent any time promoting my EFA profile in any way. But since the EFA is such a highly respected network, authors look there to find an editor, and they find me. The networking and educational opportunities with the EFA are limitless. If you're serious about building your career as a freelance editor, you *must* join the EFA.

*LinkedIn*
We talked about LinkedIn in the last chapter and determined that we can use LinkedIn as a kind of online resume. But beyond simply connecting to professionals through LinkedIn as social media, connecting to other editors, publishing gurus, and authors on LinkedIn is a great way to grow your network. One aspect of LinkedIn

that can potentially expand your editing business network is LinkedIn groups. As you establish your niche, join LinkedIn groups that fit that niche. Engage with members in the group, offering value and not simply promoting yourself.

*Writing Groups & Author Communities*
Writing groups are everywhere. No matter where you live, you can probably find a writing group that meets for workshopping and writing events. You want to connect with authors? Attend some writers group meetings in your area. But don't just go in with a business card and start selling your services. Go to the writing groups with your own work to workshop and critique. Open yourself up to authors in the same vulnerable way that you want your authors to open up to you. Connect with authors in your area on a personal level and then make your services known and available to them.

*Referrals*
Did you notice the one thing that almost all of these have in common? That's right: referrals! A freelance editor's career relies on referrals. If you receive a referral from a fellow freelance editor, be sure to discuss whether or not that referrer expects you to pay them a referral rate. Generally, the referral rate between editors is around 10% of the service fees. As a freelancer, your time is precious, and the minutes you spend corresponding with an author who you eventually refer to another editor is time you would like to be compensated for. Remember that when you receive referrals from colleagues.

I also encourage you to request referrals from your best clients. If you worked with a particularly fantastic client, ask that they pass on your contact information to any friends/colleagues of theirs who may be writing similar books. Gathering testimonials is another way to gain credibility and name recognition and find more clients in your niche.

Now, there is one thing about the editorial world I want to lean on here, and it may be something you haven't heard from other editors.

This is the truth as I see it: **Freelance editing isn't a competition.** You will never "lose" a project to a fellow editor. Editing is about relationships. Let's lift one another up and enjoy our shared greatness.

That is why I will never tell a fellow editor to go on a bidding site to find work—even when you're first starting out. Those websites force freelancers to compete to *lower* their value and discount their experience just to get a project. They encourage self-sabotage as a way of doing life and business. I never want to subject myself to that, and I never want any of my fellow editors to devalue themselves either!

There is *so much room* at the top for every individual editor. No two editors have the same knowledge and experience. No two editors will have the same *exact* niche. No two editors can work every bit as well with one particular author. There is always one who fits while the rest don't, no matter what the project is.

I've had projects I was *convinced* were perfect for me that went to other editors who share some of my expertise. But no matter how I felt like I lost in a "competition," after a while, the reason for the choice became clear. In one instance, it turned out that though the subject matter of the book itself was right down my alley, the client was unwilling to pay my rates and would have been fighting me on them for the duration of the project. That is *not* a fun experience, friends. So that project went to another editor instead—one who charged less. And you know what? That's OK! That editor was the right fit for that client and project and I wasn't.

Instead of feeling defeated that I didn't get a project, I can be grateful for the projects I have and continue to get that are the perfect fit, like Ned Pelger, author of *Great Sex, Christian Style* and blogger at GreatSexChristianStyle.com (both of which I edited and designed). I consider myself a successful editor because of the amazing authors I've worked with, and I don't consider it a failure that I've been turned down for some projects in my career.

I can't wait to see you all up here at the top, and I hope I have the privilege to reach out my own hand out to help you get here. We aren't in competition. We're a community. Reach out to me online! Let's be pals! Let's help one another succeed!

Your network can help you get in the right circles for finding work. Our clients have to trust us in order to be willing to hand over their personal or professional property to us to work on, and personal referrals from our established network is key to that. Beyond your network, you'll get projects when you "hunt" for them. More on being a freelance hunter next.

# 13

## Pricing & Finding Work

So you know the services you want to offer and you know where you fit in the editing world genre-wise. But how do you price your services?

I do a lot of emailing back and forth with potential editing clients, and I've found that a common question has to do with the price of editorial services. While every freelance editor is different—with different education, skills, experience, and certifications—there are certain industry standards for pricing, which we should all follow as a general rule. The EFA has a comprehensive list of price ranges for freelance editing services on the Editorial Freelancer's Association website, but I created my own formula for determining how much I charge for the editing services I provide. My general hourly fee is $50. Now, if you go to the EFA's price list, you'll notice that the price ranges for the different types of editing that I offer are set at an industry standard as follows:
- Developmental editing: $45-55 per hour
- Basic copyediting: $30-40 per hour
- Heavy copyediting: $40-50 per hour
- Proofreading: $30-35 per hour

You can see that I'm generally right in the midrange for pricing per hour for most types of editing, but let's talk about the two services it appears I overcharge for: basic copyediting and proofreading. I charge $50 per hour for copyediting and proofreading. I don't lower my hourly rate to complete those types of editing. You might be saying, "That means you're overcharging by almost $20 an hour!"

Actually, I'm not.
- For basic copyediting, standards show that an editor can complete between five and 10 manuscript pages per hour.
- For proofreading, standards show that an editor can complete between nine and 13 manuscript pages per hour.

So for $30-40 an hour, a copyeditor charging industry standards can only complete between 5-10 pages per hour. But I charge $50, and I stay firm on my hourly charge because I generally complete *12-15* pages per hour for basic copyediting. Same for proofreading: I can complete between *15-20* pages per hour of proofreading. I know my rate of work because I've been doing this for years. I've worked in my niche and outside of my niche...and I've learned that I work best on manuscripts in my niche (creative manuscripts in the genres of fiction, creative nonfiction—including memoir, and anything in the religious studies genre). I've learned I work best at home or in a public building with a good internet connection, little distraction and noise, and plenty of coffee.

Now, look one more time at that pricing table at the number of pages per hour ranges for developmental editing and heavy copyediting:
- Developmental Editing: 1-5 pages per hour

- Heavy Copyediting: 2-5 pages per hour

I charge $50 per hour for both services, but here's where my rates are at an even better value than industry standards:
- I can complete between 6-8 pages per hour of developmental editing.
- I can complete between 8-10 pagers per hour of heavy copyediting.

That means in the $45-55 per hour range for heavy copyediting, I not only charge the middle amount ($50), I also deliver at least double the number of pages in that hour. How do I do that? My reading speed has increased dramatically over the years, I am able to key into an author's writing style and common errors quickly and fix them, and I have established a process by which I work (and I've shared some of my tips throughout this book) that allows me to edit at a faster pace while still being thorough and creative. For every few years of experience I put under my belt, I ask myself a handful of questions about the price I charge for my services:

1. What is different about my experience since 2-3 years ago?
2. What have I done to enhance my education and career development in the last 2-3 years?
3. How have my skills changed and improved over the last 2-3 years?
4. What are the industry standards now?
5. What about my freelance career has changed or been altered by industry standards, the publishing world, and my own ventures?

In 2016, I evaluated my per hour price. I had just completed my Master's degree from Duke Divinity School. I had begun working as an adjunct professor teaching students how to edit and publish two publications for the school. I accepted contract work for the college alumni magazine doing proofreading, had copyedited for clients throughout my Master's degree in genres of fiction and memoir, and I edited multiple graduate academic papers in the field of religious studies. I had worked for established authors and first-time authors alike and gained knowledge and experience in every skill I wrote on in the first section of this book. I was writing more, editing faster, and soaking up editorial, writing, and design skills like a sponge. In 2015, I charged $35 per hour for all services. Answering the questions above with my experience, education and career development, my skills, and the way in which the world of freelance editing had shifted over the last few years, I came to the conclusion that I would raise my per hour price to $50. A few years from now, perhaps when I reach the 10-year mark, I will reevaluate, and I may raise my prices even further, but I will continue to base my hourly rate on those questions.

As a new freelancer, you won't be able to charge $50 per hour right out of the gate. But *please* do not go to the far end of cheap just to land gigs. If you want to be full-time editor, you must, MUST, be seeking out *clients*—not fluffy, busy-work projects—and that means you must charge within industry standards. No one will take you seriously as an editor if you charge $10 per hour or less.

I started at $25 per hour my first year in the field, and I was told by countless clients and fellow editors that I wasn't charging enough. I charged $25 for one year before upping it to $30 and eventually to $35 before I made the shift to $50 per hour. While I perhaps wasn't being paid what my time and work was actually worth for the first few years, I did my job well and was able to gain life-long clients and begin the referral system in the process. The authors I worked for in my first five years of freelance editing have come back to me with new books, have connected me with their friends who are writing books, and have supported me in my own writing. You're building your network here. Let everything in your business—including your pricing—work toward that goal.

Another thing to consider when pricing your services is what other options your potential clients have and what those options would cost your potential clients. Take CreateSpace (now part of KDP) for example. CreateSpace offered copyediting services ($160 for 10,000 words), more in depth editing with line editing services ($210 for 10,000 words), interior formatting services ($249-349), cover design ($399), marketing services ($249), and other services that allowed authors to just pay the fees and get their books published. Altogether, an author going through the CreateSpace paid services from editing to marketing would cost less than if an author pays you to do it for them. However, as a former copyeditor/line editor for a company CreateSpace employed to complete the copyediting and line editing services detailed above, I can tell you that the CreateSpace route is *not* the most personable, the most thorough, or the most community-oriented route. Many, *many* authors want an editor they can talk to and get to know. Many—or *most*—authors want to feel like their editor is working alongside them to create a book readers want to read. They will be willing to make an investment in your services because they seek more than just to get the editing and publishing completed on their book. They don't want to figure it all out themselves, but they want more involvement than simply uploading a document and approving it with a faceless, voiceless, emotionless platform. Just remember that in order to "steal" those authors away from CreateSpace-type options, your ability to assist authors and your experience doing so must qualify the price you're wanting to charge them. The questions above will help you set those rates and give you every ability to defend them.

### Finding Work

Once you settle on the price you will charge for each service you offer, you have to start seeking out available projects. First, make sure you have a classy, clean, and, *obviously*, well-edited resume on hand that details your education, professional development, and any editing experience you have. This book is in the genre of "professional development," but just reading it doesn't really count as professional development. If you can afford it, find one or two online classes to purchase (these make great Christmas present ideas for newbie freelancers) and list those on your resume. I took a class called Editorial Bootcamp that was vital to my business formation and was a great addition to my resume.

With resume in hand, start reaching out to potential clients. Join the EFA and respond to job posts that match your skills, niche, and price of services. The EFA job board has been *the* place where I find new clients in my editing niche. Depending on your niche, you may find projects or contract work on job boards like Monster or Indeed. If you plan to offer writing services, check out blogging job boards. Contact the managing editors at journals or publications in your niche about possible contract work. Contact publishing companies and Indie publishers. Contact editorial services corporations. Every writer needs an editor, so contact any entities in your niche and in your general location.

No matter what kind of services you want to offer, you're going to have to go on the hunt to find them. Your clients—especially in your first few years as a freelancer—won't come to you. You have to go to them. Seek them out. "Hunt" them down (too strong? I can't always tell). I know better than anyone how self-sabotage and lack of confidence can derail you here. You'll probably find yourself thinking, *I'm going to come off too pushy or self-important. No one is going to want to hire me. I'll just wait for something to come to me.* Well, if you act on that (or rather DON'T act), you'll never be a successful freelancer. Think of yourself as a qualified expert. Never discount your humanities education and professional and personal development. Say aloud every single day, "I am a professional editor. I am talented and skilled in editing in my niche, (insert niche here), and authors want to work with me. I am successful and driven." We call that a verbal affirmation. Never underestimate its power.

Set aside every hesitation to reach out to any company, author, or publication you want to edit for and rock your introduction. Any author would be lucky to work with you. Tell yourself that every day. Do it. I'm serious.

*My Top Tips for Getting New Clients*
I've sought out tons of potential contract work and editing clients, and my success has come down to two

things: editing tests and sample edits. Both the editing test and a sample edit are ways of illustrating your skills for your potential client. Simply by expressing your willingness to take an editing test or complete a sample edit, you are telling your potential clients that you can and will demonstrate your expertise to them prior to being hired. We will talk about editing tests in the next chapter in more detail. Here are my thoughts on sample edits.

A sample edit is a short excerpt from an author's manuscript on which the editor shows his or her editing services. I charge between $30 and $50 for a sample edit (depending on length), and the value both I and my inquiring authors receive more than quadruples that amount in time and money. As my former editorial assistant, Ethan, said, "The sample edit is the trust fall of editing."

A sample edit does four things:
1. allows me, the editor, to get a sense of the author's voice, writing style, and project;
2. allows the author to see my work, style, and proficiency;
3. gives both the author and me peace of mind about entering into a business transaction; and
4. is an excellent tool for estimating project cost and determining the type of editing needed.

I listed the sample edit's ability to give me a sense of an author's voice, writing style, and project first because even more vital than showing my editing skills is making sure I am a good fit for the project itself. I know my skills and experience. I can list the books I've worked on and the types of editing I've done and how long I've done them, but beyond those skills, I can tell whether or not I fit with a client's writing style and project by completing a sample edit and corresponding with the author. I need to know whether or not I want to commit to "catching" the project and asking for it to "fall" my way. It is sometimes called "sticking to your niche." I stick to creative manuscripts in humanities genres—specializing in religious studies. But there are times when I'm still not quite the right fit for a book in my particular niche. A sample edit helps me decide if the project is right for me as an editor. Remember, this is a business built on relationships.

The sample edit allows me to show my grammar and editing style and my ability to edit into an author's voice and style. When I return a completed sample edit, the author has a personalized insight into the services I can complete for his or her manuscript. It is like getting a freebie of substantial value that includes a guarantee of professional work. The author gets that insight and can even compare sample edits and choose the editor whose work they like the best. The sample edit lets the author know whether or not they can trust me and let the project "fall" to me.

The peace of mind a sample edit provides is crucial when you're talking about over $1,000 in cost of services being exchanged. The author needs to know that I can do the job I say I can do. The sample edit shows that. I need to know that I'm a good fit for the project. The sample edit lets me decide that. If I complete a sample edit and feel like I'm a good fit for the book and the author sees my work and can feel confident in my abilities and services, I'm more likely to trust that the author will pay me in full and the author is more likely to trust that his or her investment will be worth the cost. I'm able to trust that the author will trust me and fall, and the author is able to trust that I will do the catching. Boom. Successful trust fall.

Finally, the sample edit allows me to better estimate how long a project will take to complete and what type of editing it requires. From the sample edit I can see common errors, I can tell whether a manuscript is ready for copyediting or needs developmental work before copyediting, and I can give a cost of editing estimation based on the total page count for the project and the amount of time it took me to complete the sample edit. The sample edit allows me to get a better sense of the project and the services I will need to complete for the manuscript and to convey that to my author.

When completing a sample edit, take your time and be as thorough as possible. Read through your edits at least twice. Make comments on areas you were unsure of or that you would like more clarification on should you be hired to complete the project. Also, make note of it if you think a manuscript needs a type of editing the author didn't ask you to demonstrate to them in the sample edit. If any questions come up that must have an answer in order for you to do a thorough sample edit, email the client and ask. Also, complete sample edits in a timely manner. If the sample is fewer than 10 pages, you should take no more than two work days to complete it and return it to your client. No matter the length of the sample edit I'm working on, I always do my best to return it to my client within one week from the day I receive it.

You may remember I said my network has been a huge source of work for me. I meant that. But NEVER have I asked for a fellow editor to kick "excess" work my way. Never. That's hella rude. You may not think it is until you're the editor being asked for that, but think about it: Imagine you're an established freelance editor and you have just begun having around half of your clients come to you rather than you having to seek them out. You're working full-time, but you're not so busy that you have to turn multiple projects away (and I don't know of a single editor who actually has to do that). You get a message from a new freelancer that says, "Hey, if you get extra work that you could throw my way, I would appreciate it." Um, what? No. You had to put in the work to get to where you are, and every other editor should (and CAN) also. If you get that from a newbie editor when you're a few years along, send them a link to this book on Amazon and say, "Get to work." As a newbie, don't ever ask for extra work. Put in the hard work to hunt for projects and establish yourself. Hustle. Nose to the grindstone. How many other ways can I say, "JUST DO THE THING?" I have that phrase written on my calendar and a white board in my home office. Just. Do. The. Thing.

In the next chapter, we will talk about how editing tests can further demonstrate your expertise and land clients for you.

# 14

## Editing Tests

I know. I say "Test" and you cringe. As a humanities major, your final tests were probably essay exams, or maybe you had mostly final papers and projects. But as freelance editors, you might be asked to take editing tests to show your proficiency in grammar, punctuation, word choice, and types of editing.

In general, you will only be asked to take an editing test if you're attempting to work for editing services companies, publishing companies, academic institutions, or established publications. If the company or group has a list of freelancers they like to work with, being added to that list requires that they can see your expertise firsthand.

**What to Expect**
Grammar, punctuation, word choice, style guide adherence for citations, developmental editing, comments, editorial letters, track changes proficiency, Microsoft Word formatting proficiency, editing for consistency, capitalization rules, hyphenation, abbreviation, commonly misused words: all are possible topics for testing. But you *absolutely do not* need to memorize every grammar rule, every style guide, and every preference for hyphenation and abbreviation.

If you have already decided you want to be an editor, you know you have a talent for noticing errors. Rely, then, on your basic understanding and learn how to find the rules for anything you don't know off the top of your head. Embrace the Google. Turn to Grammar Girl for remote grammar rules and easy ways to remember them. Grammar Girl taught me an easy way to remember the difference between "like" and "such as," and for that I am eternally grateful. In the chapter on Style Guides you learned how to use any guide; if the company you're testing for uses a particular guide, you'll be able to quickly find the rules you need to make the necessary edits on the test.

You'll discover that the editing tests you take include purposeful sections. Each company will have its own editing preferences and will work with its own specific set of rules they adhere to and rules they break. Some companies will test heavily for style guide knowledge and use while others will focus on the type of editing itself (copyediting, developmental editing, etc.). You should be able to expect that the editing test will match the job description you are applying for. If you don't fit the description, don't ask to take the test.

**Before You Get Into the Editing Test Stage**
One thing is key here, and it is the same thing I continually emphasize throughout this training manual: Do not try to do it all! You need to be as picky about the companies you work for as they are about the editors they hire. If you don't really like to work with MLA style, don't apply to a company that requires it. If you prefer developmental editing over proofreading, don't apply for a position as a proofreader and then poke your

eyes out during the proofreading test. The companies you are looking to work for and the types of editing skills and knowledge they will test for *must* match your preferences and skills. Do a little research before you apply. Does the company publish the type/genre of books that I particularly enjoy reading? Is this company looking for the kind of editing services I provide? Does this company use the style guide I'm most familiar with?

You should be able to answer those questions just by digging around on the company's website, but what happens when you apply for a position, receive the editing test, and realize you are not the right editor for the job? Surely you can't just fail to complete the test and take your name out of the running? Actually, that is *exactly* what you should do. If you find yourself a poor fit for a company or position based on the test you receive, contact the managing editor or the person who administered the test. You can use this format:

*Dear <u>Managing Editor of Such-and-such-publishers</u>,*

*Upon reviewing the content of the editing test, I realize that I am not the kind of editor you are looking for at this juncture. I specialize in <u>a, b, and c</u> editing services rather than <u>e, f, and g</u>. I appreciate the opportunity, but I would like to withdraw my application in order to focus on editing projects in my niche.*
    *Sincerely,*
    <u>*Me*</u>

Trust me: managing editors will respect the knowledge you have of your skills and abilities, and they will appreciate that you did not waste their time by taking a test on types of editing that you weren't able to excel at.

And who knows: they might even be kind enough to point you to another company that would give you work more down your alley. Be kind and respectful to other people—authors and fellow editors alike. It will take you straight to the top.

# Part 3: Getting into the Groove

# 15

## Editor's Letters

It's time to talk about what happens after you complete an editing project as you're getting into the groove of this freelance life. What can you do to impress and keep clients (besides demonstrating your incredible editing skills)? One of my favorite ways to summarize my editing expertise while also opening up the door for continued communication with my authors is the editor's letter.

An editor's letter is a descriptive explanation of all the common errors in your client's text and direction on how you fixed those errors. An editor's letter has different sections for types of editing and types of errors. By reading the editor's letter, your client should be able to see your editing process in clear, non-editor terms. If you are completing more than one type of editing on a manuscript, I suggest you include the editor's letter following the most extensive editing process you completed, whether that be developmental or copyediting.

I don't always send an editor's letter, and my decision whether or not to do so depends on my client correspondence during the project duration. If I have gotten to know my client through a continuous email correspondence chain, I don't usually send a letter. But if I haven't been able to connect as personally as I like to with a client, I can use the editor's letter to get a little deeper into that relationship. It's all about the potential for future referrals! An editor's letter is a great way to build massive trust and mutual respect between editor and author.

We'll discuss in the next chapter how to use general correspondence via email in lieu of an editor's letter. Deciding whether to include an editor's letter also has to do with the project deadline. If I'm butting up to a strict deadline with my edits, my author likely doesn't have much time to read through and revise based on an editor's letter, so I stick with email correspondence. If I've communicated extensively with the author by email during the editing process and we've discussed common errors and talked about how I fix them, I don't include an editor's letter. But if I am working with a first-time author on a self-imposed deadline and I don't make as much connection via email as I like to, I include one. I want my first-time authors to be as informed as possible about the editing process, and an editor's letter helps me do that.

I include the same basic parts in every editor's letter: an overview of the manuscript as a whole, examples of common grammar, punctuation, syntax, and word choice errors, comments on structure, character development, plot, etc. (depending on the genre), and suggestions for beginning the revision process. Make the letter as personable as you can, but make sure to stay professional in your language.

As with any conversation about editing, I like to use the sandwich rule: sandwich any negative comments between positive ones. I always start my letter by praising the manuscript before I dive into what needs work. I then end with more praise and discuss the goal of the manuscript and where I see it fitting in the publishing world. I give suggestions on how to better appeal to an author's intended audience, other types of editing the manuscript needs before publishing, and ideas for cover designs, marketing plans, etc.

I have a template for each genre I edit most often. Check them out and feel free to use them as starting points for your own editor's letters:

## Fiction
Dear <u>Author</u>,

**Overview paragraph (describe what you think about the manuscript, using praise words as much as possible) and transition to common errors.**
It was a pleasure to edit your manuscript <u>Such and Such manuscript</u>. I enjoyed the <u>such and such characters or plot or etc.</u> and I was impressed at your use of <u>such and such</u>. The edits I made to your manuscript were mostly <u>of such and such variety</u> and I will explain the common errors below.

**Common Errors in Grammar, Punctuation, Syntax, and Word Choice (3-5 examples and explanations):**
I noticed the misuse of "that" versus "which" throughout your manuscript. Use "that" when the clause following the word is necessary to the meaning of the text. Do not use a comma with "that."

Use "which" when the clause following the word is unnecessary to the meaning of the text. Include a comma before "which."

Example:
**Incorrect**: She participated in the daily activities of the house, that included shopping and cleaning.
**Corrected**: She participated in the daily activities of the house, which included shopping and cleaning.

(The next sections are fairly self-explanatory. Comment on any of these categories that are pertinent to the manuscript you're working on.)
- **Character Development**
- **Plot/Structure**
- **World Creation**
- **Terms to Define**

**Manuscript Goals:** Does the manuscript meet the goals it set out to meet? (This is a discussion you should have with your client in your initial correspondence: *What are your publishing goals? What are you hoping to accomplish with this manuscript?*)

**Closing Paragraph** (Summarize what you discussed in this letter and end with a note of praise.)

## Memoir/Creative Nonfiction

Same first two sections as for fiction (Overview paragraph and Common errors in grammar, punctuation, syntax and word choice).

(Then, comment on any of the following sections that are pertinent to the project you're working on.)

**Narrator**
**Character Development**
**Structure**
**Citation Questions and Concerns** (How would revision help them avoid charges of libel?)

**Manuscript Goals** (Same as for fiction.)
**Closing Paragraph** (Summarize what you discussed in this letter and end with a note of praise.)


The above templates should give you a starting point for creating your own editor's letter templates that fit the genres you're working in. Now let's discuss client correspondence in more detail.

# 16

## Client Correspondence

There are good and bad, proper and improper, appropriate and inappropriate ways to correspond with potential, current, and former editing clients. I've been a member of the EFA for a few years now, and every year my $200 membership fee is more than worth the payment when I am able to land a book project by corresponding with authors on the EFA job posts. I put a lot of time and effort into responding to job posts in a way that shows my experience and education without making me seem like a grammar jerk. Here are some tips on corresponding with clients.

*EFA Job Posts*
When you join the EFA, you can opt in to receive job post emails. When you receive a post that fits your niche, you'll have the author's contact information and you will reply to the author directly. A successful job post response will demonstrate that you understand the specifics of the project and the author's needs from the job post, that you have the experience and education to match the project, and that you are willing to provide references, a resume, and any other necessary information about yourself and your experience to convince the author that you fit the project.

I always start out my job post responses by stating who I am and why I was attracted to the job post. I then describe my experience and how I fit the project. Here is an example of a winning EFA job post response email. This email is in response to a project in the religious studies genre:

*Dear Ned,*

*My name is Kathrin Herr, and I received your job post through the EFA. I am the founding editor at The Writing Mechanic—an editing services company.*

*I am a professional editor with over seven years of professional freelance editing experience, and I specialize in editing in the religious studies genre. I hold my BA in Religion from Simpson College and my MA in Christian Studies, with an emphasis in spiritual writing, from Duke Divinity School. I have worked with a number of authors in the religious studies field, and I am particularly gifted in the areas of developmental editing (editing for flow and concision) and copyediting (grammar, punctuation, syntax, etc.).*

*I am well versed in working with the* Chicago Manual of Style *(I also teach CMOS guide usage at the college level) and, if you'd be interested, The Christian Writers Manual of Style for formatting of citations. I also know all the ins and outs of self-publishing on Amazon Kindle Direct Publishing for print-on-demand and eBook. I can format your interior document for publication using both of those platforms. I am also a cover designer.*

*I am a "staunch" intersectional feminist, so my personal views seem to be in line with yours and with the work you're doing.*

*I charge $50 per hour for all types of editing. I would be happy to complete your sample edit. I can start the sample edit at any time.*

*My resume is available at your request. Please visit my website, http://www.kathrinherr.com, for more about the work I do.*

*Sincerely,*
*Kathrin Herr*

You should write an organic email response to every EFA job post. You can use the above example as a general format, but match each email response to the project at hand. It takes time to earn a client's trust, so set aside time in your weekly schedule to correspond with potential new clients—responding to job posts, emailing managing editors, etc.

> **Tip**: Don't attach your resume to the first email you send to a client. Emails with attachments are often sent to spam. Instead, add a note to the end of the email saying, "My resume is available at your request."

*Email "Cold-Calls"*
If you're wanting to get in a freelancer pool for a publishing company or publication, you'll probably have to make some email "cold-calls" to managing editors. Just like cold calls for sales and marketing, an email

"cold-call" is a form of uninitiated contact, so be as polite, professional, and respectful as possible. Find the contact information for the managing editor or the marketing director of the publishing company and craft a polite email inquiring about how they handle the editing of their publications. Ask if they use contractors or a freelance pool to complete editing projects. Mention that you're happy to complete any editing tests they might have and that you will provide your references upon their request.

Fifty-percent of the time you won't hear anything back. If you feel like you are a perfect fit for a publisher or publication that didn't respond to your email, find the email address for another member of the staff and initiate contact with that person instead. The other half of the time you'll get an email back and they will be interested in working with you or they'll politely decline because they do their editing in house.

*Cold Pitches*
If you want to offer your copywriting services to companies, you'll probably need to "cold pitch." This will take time. In order to cold pitch to a company, for editing their website content or publications specifically and for writing for them, you need to spend time looking over their current text and taking extensive notes. Many companies do not seek out editors for their websites or marketing materials because they don't recognize their need. What you need to be able to do is show how you could improve their text...without coming across as snobby or full of yourself. Do your best to pick out and explain what you see as the company's message and share how you would be able to improve the reach of that message by editing or writing for them. Keep their

concerns at the forefront of the conversation. What do they need? How can you provide a solution for them with your own skills and experience? Use the sandwich rule and praise more than you point out shortcomings. Make them see that you recognize their value and then convince them that you want to help make that value even greater.

*General Tips*
Write every email in a formal, yet approachable voice. Make sure you pay attention to the needs of your clients and demonstrate that you are willing and able to meet their needs. If the client would like to discuss the project over the phone, make sure you make yourself available to talk over the phone. If they want to talk over Skype, get a Skype account.

Have confidence in your experience and demonstrate that in your correspondence. Make sure your potential or current client will recognize you as an expert in your field. Be careful not to come off too haughty, though. Demonstrate confidence without showing off. Have an editing friend (perhaps a member of your professional network) read through your correspondence (particularly your cold-call emails) before you send them and ask for feedback on your writing voice. Would they want to respond to you if they received that email?

Even consider going old school and writing a handwritten note to the companies or clients you're trying to work with. Few people take the time to connect with a handwritten note, and it may set you apart in their minds. Just make sure you have decent handwriting. No chicken scratch, please.

*Email Correspondence with Current Clients*
If you work with your clients mostly by email (which is what I do), you might find it unnecessary to write an editor's letter at the end of a project. You may be writing back and forth throughout the project asking questions and getting feedback. If that's the case, remember to always praise more than you criticize—even in an email! Make sure your clients know how thankful you are to be working on their book...don't make them think they are a terrible writer by picking them apart without building them back up. Your authors will become repeat customers if you develop a relationship based on mutual respect. If you choose not to cultivate that respect with a more formal editor's letter, make sure you cultivate it in your daily correspondence instead.


*Responding to a "No" Client*
There will be times in which you have to respond to a potential client who wants to hire you but whom you do not want to work with. A client may be a "no" client if they question your fees, have unreasonable expectations of your work (or of editing in general), or if their project clashes too much with your personal ethics. When you identify that you're corresponding with a "no" client, craft a polite but firm email to end your working relationship. Some good points to make could be, "Your project does not really fit my work niche," "I am not the best editor for this project," or "Our writing/editing styles do not match, and I would suggest that you seek editing services elsewhere," and include some ideas of where to find another editor. Don't leave a door open to a "no" client. If you have a bad feeling about a project, end the working relationship. Just be sure to retain your professionalism in the process.

*How to Deal with "Losing" a Project*
It's something we all have to deal with at one point or another, and it always sucks. You'll have a client who says, "I want you to work on my project," but then comes back a week later saying, "I decided to go another way." That truly sucks. Nothing makes you question your skills more than an editing "breakup" like that. My advice for dealing with this is to remain polite in your responses. Tell the client you understand, or perhaps ask why they changed their mind. Do not waiver on your prices if they say they went with another editor because your prices were too high. There are clients out there willing to pay your fees. You'll find them. Don't lower your standards or expectations for that kind of client. Also, remember that you are never really in competition with another editor. If a client decides to go another way, that wasn't a project for you anyways, and you'll be better off in the long run seeking out projects that are your perfect fit.


*When You Drop the Ball...*
No matter how organized you are...no matter how "on it" you are...no matter how great you've been for your entire career...there will come a time when you drop the ball. You'll have a crap week or two weeks or month. Life will get in the way and you'll miss a deadline. An important email will fall through the cracks. It WILL happen. So *when* you drop the ball, don't get defensive. Don't try to explain. Apologize and do everything you can to make it right with your client. Hopefully you will have cultivated enough mutual respect with your client beforehand and you'll be able to keep your working relationship intact through the difficulties. We have a lot on our plate as freelancers—more than a typical 9-5 or salaried job entails. We'll mess up sometimes...I

certainly have. But it's how you deal with the screw-ups...that's what you should judge yourself by. So pick the ball back up when you drop it and make it right with the client first. And don't be too hard on yourself, either.

Next we're going to talk about something all freelancers want: residual income.

# 17

## Scaling Your Editing Business & Diversifying Your Income

Editing is usually a time-for-money conversion. You are hired to edit a book, you work on the book (paid hourly or by page/word), you get paid for the work you do, and then your income from that project ends. While working your way up to fulltime freelance editing is an ideal goal, you may want to start thinking through ways to make "passive" or "residual" income from a product that you can create once and then sell repeatedly for continual income that doesn't require extra time on your part.

You can create passive income in a number of different ways. Most of the passive income sources freelance editors can do involve writing in some form. For instance, you could create an info product, such as an eBook. You could also create a class, such as a pre-recorded, online prompt writing class or webinar. If you're gifted in the social media world, you may even be able to get some affiliate sales income from other companies. Here are some suggestions for passive-income-producing products you can create in a short amount of time.

*Books & eBooks*
You could follow my lead and write a book to earn passive income! That's part of what this book is for my business—a passive income product. I wrote it once, and I don't have to write it again, but I'm able to sell it repeatedly and earn more and more income from it. I've also written eBooks for my other projects that produce a little extra income from one or two days of work.

This book took significantly longer to write. You now know exactly how to publish books on Amazon KDP, thanks to Part 1, so you'll be able to do that for your own book without having to pay someone else to do it. You can also make your eBook PDFs for sale on your website by simply setting it up to download from your website upon purchase.

Just like you would recommend for your authors' books, come up with a social media marketing strategy for your book or eBook and consider giving away a freebie with it, such as a worksheet or checklist—something that will take only a few minutes to create but that will provide value to your potential readers. You need to promote the sale of your product in order to make any real passive income from it, so use your social media best practices and schedule your posts to save time.

*Blogging for Money*
Another way to produce residual income in your editing business is through your blog and your social media platforms. Many companies will pay you an affiliate fee if you promote a product or service on your website that leads your readers to purchase said product or service. A company will provide you with your particular affiliate

link, which you can just place on your website in a strategic blog or page or post to your social media platforms. Be sure to work with companies whose products are in some way complementary to your business and services so you're sure to stay on topic with your readers. You worked hard to get your ideal readers to your website and in your social media networks. Don't push them away with affiliates that don't match your own mission and vision.

You can also allow advertisements on your website for money. If you have hundreds of thousands of readers on your website every month, which will take a while to build to but is completely attainable if you choose to work for it, you may find value in allowing advertisements. Just be warned that allowing ads may turn some readers away. If you do include ads, try to make sure they are minimally disruptive to your reading experience.

One fun way to work with companies to make residual income is to write a sponsored post for them. Companies will pay you to write a blog about their product or service and when you combine that with an affiliate link to that particular product or service, the amount of money you can continually get for writing the blog post once may be exponential.

*Webinars & Email Classes*
Would your niche of expertise and your particular experience be of value to authors who follow you on social media? Do you have a particular skill you can teach? Create a free email class in which you ask your audience to sign up with their email addresses to receive

a free training series in their inboxes once a day for 5-10 days. In those emails, mention and link to a paid webinar you record and password protect on your website. Your free email series will prime your audience to purchase access to your webinar training by providing them with value for free and convincing them that what you offer in the paid version is worth the investment. Doing this a few times on a few different topics will build up your webinar library and make passive income from it. Simply setting up automated email series in MailChimp for each email class and webinar can let you set it and forget it. The automation service is now part of the free MailChimp account.

Any of these products help you to earn passive income on something you do the work for only once. They can help you get out of the time-for-money conversion and help grow your audience and network, which will in turn land you more clients, simultaneously.

Something else you might want to consider is diversifying your income by doing something outside the publishing world for income. I'm talking about a "side-hustle."

There are a bunch of options for potential side-hustles: network marketing, product sales, one-on-one coaching, starting a small home cleaning business, etc. Just Google "Side Hustle Options" and you'll find lists of ideas.

I decided to go with network marketing for my side hustle because network marking let me continue to work as a freelancer without taking any time and energy away from my projects. And I was lucky enough to be able to add my side-hustle into my editing and writing business when I rebranded myself. Check out www.kathrinherr.com to see what I mean.

So why might it be important to diversify your income as a freelancer? Surely you've heard the saying "don't put all your eggs in one basket." Even as a freelancer working for multiple clients or publishing entities, if you only edit, you could have a time in which you have absolutely no work coming in. I've had seasons like that, and they are terrifying. Putting my income "eggs" in other baskets gives me more stability; when one "basket" is a little smaller one month, the others are still going strong or growing.

Another reason to consider diversifying your income is to avoid burnout. Eight years I've been doing this, and I can tell you there are days I would rather do ANYTHING else but edit the book manuscript on my computer screen. I've had days when I just pace around my office, do all the cleaning around the house, get lost in Netflix, even clean the toilets (gross) just to avoid getting to work because I'm just burned out. But since I've diversified my income, I get to do more different types of things (without falling into the "doing it all" as a freelancer trap) that help me avoid the burnout while still growing my income and opportunities.

Thinking about doing more than just editing? How about adding freelance writing to your services? Let's talk about why I think writing as an editor is important for more reasons than simply increased earning opportunities.

# 18

## The Writing Editor

Authors want to hire people they feel understand their issues, their desires, and their needs. If you're an editor, you should do what you can to improve your own writing and share your thoughts and ideas with your network.

Writers trust other writers because they have to do the same things. They experience the same things. They have the same frustrations. They have the same pain points. Many of them have the same goals. If you're a writer as well as an editor, you'll relate to your potential clients on a whole other level. Increased trust equals more clients in your fold.

Start with a private journal. Write something every day. Consider adding journaling to your morning routine. Sit down with your journal and your thoughts for 15 minutes every single morning and write. You can write about anything, just be sure you're not spending that time making lists of your daily tasks. Let yourself be creative for a few minutes a day.

Blogging is another simple way to get in the practice of writing. Blog once per week at a minimum, and if you have a fellow editor in your network who is doing the same thing, consider setting up an editing partnership: you edit their blogs and they edit yours. There is no need for an exchange of funds for this, and it will ensure you're both coming across professionally for your network. Blogging consistently will increase your reach and grow your network. I know you had to write papers for your degree. Dig back into your research and write about something that interests you on your blog. If it excites you enough to make you want to keep going, make it into a book and utilize your editorial network to publish it collectively.

Do you have an author, editor, or general blogger (on topic, preferably) you admire who has a blog and an established network? Ask if you can do a guest post on their website and offer to publish something of theirs on yours. This will help get your name and your writing in front of a new network of readers. The give and take of network exposure can be huge for both of your businesses. If you're working with another editor on this, be sure you are both clear on your niches and make a commitment to one another that you will not venture onto one another's "turf." If the blog you write on your colleague's website gets a client coming to you whose project is not in your niche of expertise, go overboard talking up your colleague and send them to the right place.

Are you a Pinterest hoarder? Create a board for writing prompts and exercises and collect 50 or more before you make a list of them all (including their sources!) and share them with your network. If you're particularly ambitious, write a few responses to those prompts and share your responses with your network as well.

Working on a book or eBook? Share a section of it in social media or in your writing group and ask for feedback. Be vulnerable with your own writing so your network can trust you to edit their writing.

Even writing emails and series of emails that you'll send out to your network is a form of writing that helps keep you visible and makes you more trustworthy in the eyes of your potential clients. Make sure your voice shines through your writing—remembering you don't have to be 100% grammatically correct 110% of the time...gasp. Yup. I said it. You can "get jiggy with" your grammar in emails. "Na na nana nana na. Na na nana nana." (Now that song will be stuck in your head for a year. You're welcome.)

*Freelance Writing*
If writing is one of the business services you want to offer, consider getting some training. While you might be a stellar writer, writing for money is another animal. American Writers and Artists, INC (AWAI) and the Barefoot Writer are fantastic resources for the newbie freelance writer. Both offer online classes that teach you everything from how to write a successful cold-pitch to finding writing projects and marketing your unique skills as a freelance writer. For specific training in the skills your freelance career requires, go to them. Tell them I sent you. They'll probably say, "Who?" but that's ok.

Here are just a handful of tips for establishing yourself as a freelance writer:

- Remember to stick in your genre(s) of expertise. Write what you know in the language/jargon you know. Here is where your particular humanities degree will come in handy. If you majored in religion, you're probably qualified to write on matters of theology, church history, Bible, and Christian ministry. Check out Christian companies, like Chic Fil A, or church groups or ministries, like UMCOR, and see what their writing needs might be.

- Look for projects writing about what interests you. If you write about a topic you enjoy—even if it isn't necessarily your editing specialty—you'll be more likely to do research to write about it with authority. For example, I wrote for The Grow Network, an online network of homesteaders and home-grown-food experts. Sure, when I started I was somewhat more comfortable editing a theology book than a book on expert gardening and raising livestock, but the topic of homesteading interests me and I happy devour books on the subject. After a while, my topic of interest became a new area of expertise for me and I'm able to write about it from a place of personal experience and authority.
- Combine as many aspects of online writing as you can for maximum earning potential. If you're writing blogs for a website with your name on them, see if they have an affiliate program you can join and put the links (with a blog on the same topic) on your website. Ask if you can either repost the blogs you write or include excerpts with links to their website for maximum exposure. If you've been working with a company for a while, ask if they would pay you to write a sponsored post on your website for one of their products.

*Ghostwriting*

We talked about ghostwriting in chapter 2, but let's talk more about this potential service here. Ghostwriting is different from regular freelance writing because your task is to write in the voice of someone else. If you participated in any kind of journalism in your undergraduate studies, you may be surprised how amazing you can be at ghostwriting (and if you're still in school, I encourage you to join the school newspaper! Write for the lifestyle or features sections. They'll be right down your alley!). To be a good ghostwriter, you need to learn how to interview people and do research on them and how to adopt their voice in your own writing. A good journalist (especially one who writes features!) is able to write *about* someone or something convincingly. That's only a hop-skip-and-a-jump away from ghostwriting, and since you're already an editor, you have an extra foot in the game.

Some clients you might ghostwrite for will give you some content they've written for the book and you'll be writing the rest of it or structuring it and writing to fill in the gaps. If that's the case, you'll be able to act as a super involved developmental editor.

Ghostwriting can be a really fun way to break up your usual editing projects—the ones where you're just reading and fixing errors—with a more creative way of thinking and creating. Live inside of someone else's head for a while! It will probably make you an even better editor and freelance writer.

If you're a humanities grad and a wannabe editor, you're a writer. Don't ever lose that ability or get out of practice when you're trying to establish yourself as an editor.

Write and edit every single work day and before long both of those skills and your subject areas of expertise will expand and you'll get paid a full-time salary to write and read...if only that were the case in college, am I right?!

# 19

## A Day in the Editing Life

To close out this freelance editor training guide, let's talk about what your daily life will look like when you become a freelance editor. Working from home sounds great—even ideal—but it is anything but *simple*. Aside from the need to set up your home office, you'll probably find it difficult to get used to scheduling out your time, keeping all of your online media up-to-date, and building to and retaining full-time editing status.

An issue every freelancer will run into at one point or another is keeping an ideal work atmosphere intact. If you work at home, you'll probably run into any of these issues: failing Wi-Fi, at-home interruptions like roommates or spouses, pets, friends, and family members assuming you're available because you're at home, or other distractions in the form of an at-home to-do list. If you work at a remote location, such as a coffee shop or library, you many run into issues like spending too much money on food and drinks, loud and/or distracting people or events taking place in the public space, failing Wi-Fi, or an unprotected/shared internet connection.

The key to working well at home is establishing a routine and planning for all contingencies (e.g., If your home Wi-Fi fails, how will you work without it or how will you spend the least amount of time fixing it?). The key to working well at a remote location is being flexible and adapt to changing circumstances (e.g., If the atmosphere becomes too loud to concentrate, make sure you have music that you can work to and crank it up in your headphones. And remember your headphones!). In either space, make sure you have a good desk and supportive work chair, decent lighting so your eyes don't get tired, and a source of power for your computer and other needed electronics. Once you have your work space established and your contingency plans in place, work on scheduling out your time.

Remember that you're only getting paid for the hours you're working on *paying* projects, but you will have to complete unpaid tasks to keep your freelance career going. Schedule in time to return and compose emails, respond to job posts, write connection/inquiry emails, check in with former clients, schedule and engage on social media, write blogs, and spend time online or on the phone to build your network.

Budget your time like you budget your money. If you don't budget all your cents, they'll disappear in the cracks somewhere. The same goes for your time. Schedule your minutes so you don't lose them to the abyss of social media or email.

It will take time to learn how long each task takes you, and you'll get faster at completing each task the more you work from home, but here is a basic idea of how long each task should take you:

- *Responding to emails*: no more than 30 minutes per day.

- *Responding to job posts, crafting emails, or checking in with former clients*: no more than 30 minutes per day. (double that if you're reaching out to a potential client outside your warm market)
- *Scheduling & Engaging on Social Media*: no more than 30 minutes per day.
- *Writing & Editing Your Blogs*: no more than one hour per day.
- *Online Network building*: no more than 30 minutes per day.

All of your unpaid tasks should take no more than three hours of your work time. I am always looking for ways to save time on social media and online networking. I put a cap on my email time each day so that I don't get sucked in to the email web and waste tons of time. If you don't get to a particular email on Monday, it can probably wait until Tuesday. If it is of vital importance, respond to it first and push less-vital correspondence to the next day. I also find that I write blogs faster if I schedule out at least of month-worth of blog topics at a time, which I'm working on doing toward the end of each month to prepare for the next month; that way I have my attention on a particular topic and can begin crafting blogs in my head when I'm driving or waiting in line (doing other everyday things). When I take the time to write my weekly blog post, then, I'm ready to write and it comes out quickly and easily.

Organization is *key* to successfully working from home. Don't use the excuse that you're unorganized. You can learn to be organized. You will not be a very successful editor if you let emails, projects, or networking opportunities slip through the cracks because you're not organized enough to keep track of everything. Make lists, set reminders and alarms, write on a calendar, keep a planner, or post sticky notes around your work space. Do whatever you need to do to keep your projects, clients, networking, and career development tasks straight. I spent way too much time setting up MailChimp email automation, designing (and fighting) my website, and learning social media quirks. Don't make that mistake. Set your stuff up at the beginning, and only spend time *optimizing* it all later on. So much of this business is trial and error and adjusting, but setting up your basic structure in all of your necessary areas of business shouldn't take a year. Be efficient with it and use the fact that you aren't getting paid to do that work as motivation to find the quickest ways to complete those tasks.

I consider full-time work to consist of 5, 8-hour work days a week, but remember, that's eight hours of PAID time. You'll need another few hours of unpaid work time in there as well. During my long editing shifts, I like to use a 2-hours on, 15-min off pattern. In your 8-hour work time, try working for two hours straight, and then take a 15-minute break to get up and do something active to get your blood pumping; and no, walking to the fridge doesn't count. Do some calisthenics, put on a yoga video on YouTube (I recommend DoYogaWithMe), or go for a jog around the block. Get your blood pumping so you don't fall into the dreaded "desk job" routine, complete with extra pounds of fat and the promise of heart disease. You may also want to carve up your paid tasks work time into your various services. If you established that you want 50% of your income to come from copyediting books, spend 50% of your work time (4 hours) every day on copyediting projects. The same goes for any of your other services. This is also a good way to tell if you need to hunt a little harder for projects in one of your areas of service. If you want to spend 30% (2 hours and 20 minutes a day) of your work time on freelance writing projects but only have enough work to spend one hour on it a day, hunt for more writing projects.

Want to plan out your day as a freelancer? Check out Appendix C for my Freelancer's Day Planning Worksheet.


*Setting Your Intentions*
Freelancers have to do one thing really well just to be a freelancer at all: We *must* be very good at being intentional. In *The Miracle Morning*, Hal Elrod talks about how vital it is to set your intentions constantly. If you need to get up earlier, set your intentions clearly in your head the night before and take the action steps necessary to actually get up earlier. That might mean using Hal's Snooze Buster tips, like putting your alarm clock across the room, and prepping at night so you can make getting up in the morning easier. If you need to apply for more editing projects, set your intentions to apply for one new project a day and take the action steps necessary to accomplish that task. That might mean setting up alerts on job sites for editing gigs, making a list of contacts in your network who might have leads on projects or be willing to connect you to their friends, or spending more time on your social media and website strategy to get more people coming to you for your services. If we aren't *intentional* with the manner in which we work and use our time (both in an out of the

office), we'll lose it to self-doubt, procrastination, and laziness.

*Tips for Living Well in the Editing/Writing Life*
These should be common knowledge and part of our everyday lives already, but as recent college students and then as freelancers, I know we don't take the following advice all that often. We know we should eat healthy and drink plenty of water, but we rarely follow-through on our New Year's Resolutions for being healthier.

I'm as guilty as you are of shirking on my health, so let's make a commitment together to take care of our bodies so we can live healthy freelance lives.

Here are some basic tips:
- Limit your intake of sugar, dairy, processed foods, and wheat.
- Drink around half of your body weight in ounces of water every day to maintain hydration—all before 3 PM if possible (so you aren't up peeing half the night).
- Drink water first thing in the morning to get your body detoxing.
- Stretch regularly to release lactic acid and improve flexibility. Sitting in a work chair with your arms up on the keyboard can make for stiff joints.
- Exercise at least three times a week for 30-40 minutes. Do some combination of cardio and strength training.
- Get a bit of sunlight whenever you can. Go for walks outside on your 15 minute breaks every two hours of work to soak up your vitamin D, or

gift yourself a sun lamp to have in your work space. Depression is a real thing, and editors can struggle with it if they are low on vitamin D.
- Set your priorities often. Consider re-setting them weekly. Write them down in order of importance. At the end of the week, go back and see how your time spent on each thing reflected or contradicted your priorities list. You can't do it all, remember? You can't, and I don't think you should try. Prioritize your tasks and make your time reflect that.
- Take breaks. If you were working a regular 9-5 gig, you'd be entitled by union rules to a 15 minute break every hour and a 30 minute break every four or more. Take those 15 minute breaks every two hours as a minimum. Let your brain rest, get your body moving, and avoid burnout.
- You won't necessarily be able to afford an expensive getaway when you're first starting out, but planning even a short vacation to somewhere within short driving distance can be a great motivator for getting various projects done. When you do take an extended break on vacation, I recommend that you turn off all email notifications (even put in an automated response informing those who email you of your return date). Schedule out some social media posts to go out when you're on vacation, and be sure to respond to any comments when you get back. But take a *real* break.
- Along with that, don't be afraid to take a day off. You would most likely have a real weekend off if you were working a regular 9-5 job, so schedule that out for yourself. Take that time off.

There is no reason you should have to work seven days a week just to keep afloat if you're optimizing your work time and spending 1-2 hours a day on non-paid, lead producing tasks.
- Spend time working on YOU, not just working. Hal Elrod, life coach and author of *The Miracle Morning*, says you have to work on yourself first before you can change your life and reach the level of success you're wanting to achieve. You have to first *become* the person you need to be to create the success and lifestyle you truly want.
- Finally, rely on community support. Fill your social media feeds with people who inspire you—other editors who are living the good life and who are transparent with how they got to where they are. If (I mean WHEN) you need help, ask for it. Don't be afraid to ask for help; I can almost guarantee you at least one of us has been where you are right now and we want to help because someone helped us. (That was my whole reason for writing this book. I want to help new editors because someone helped me.)

*Money*

A quick note about the money thing. You will be living paycheck to paycheck for a while when you're starting out, and to be honest, I'm still living that way. But budgeting your money can help relieve some of those money worries. Have a plan for how you're going to pay your bills (including your student loans...yeah, I try to forget about those too...) and fill in the cracks with some serious hustle when necessary. Plan a month ahead, and work on establishing an emergency fund (1-3 months of expenses).

If you have debt (student loans, credit card debt, etc.), build toward being able to pay the minimum plus 10% on every payment you make. Then, keep another 10% of any "extra" income aside for doing something fun. Also, use Dave Ramsey's the snowball rule for paying off your debt: pay off the smallest debt completely, then roll that monthly payment into paying off the next largest debt, and so on until all debts are paid off. I also love the "Green Gap" technique by Dr. Troy of *Oola*. Evaluate how much you spend and how much you make (just remember you'll probably not be 100% certain on the income portion all the time...or any of the time), and any amount left over of your monthly income after expenses is your "green gap." Dr. Troy recommends you take 10% of that green gap and give yourself a little lifestyle boost or reward. Then, take 45% of the rest and pay off a little more debt and the other 45% and invest in something that can start making you some passive income.

Money can be a difficult thing to manage for some of us, but if we don't budget our money and our time, we will never truly succeed as freelancers. You can do it. You have my vote of confidence, sis.

*I Wish I Would Have Started This Earlier in My Career...*
I've mentioned *The Miracle Morning* a handful of times throughout this book. I also talked about *Oola*. These are just two of the books I've read and followed teachings from to improve my life as a freelancer. For a long time, I thought I had to work on improving everything in my life at the same time. I thought to get the life I wanted—with the freelancing success I desired—I had to work on everything I wanted to change at the same time. But what *Oola* and *The Miracle Morning* taught me is that in order

to change my life, I have to work on myself and improve myself first.

So I started reading personal development books like *Girl, Wash Your Face* by Rachel Hollis. I started listening to podcasts when I was exercising or while driving. I worked on my personal health by elevating my exercise plan, eating healthier food, upping my water intake, focusing on my stress relief practices, and continuing my journaling practice. I started practicing yoga and taking supplements and therapeutic grade essential oils. And even though I had a list longer than this book of tasks to accomplish, and an even LONGER list of things I wanted to try implementing to increase my website traffic and get more clients, working on *myself first* was the single best thing I could do for my business success.

My best advice for new freelancers is to, yes, have your task list, have your goals, read plenty of professional development articles and books. Read tutorials. Do everything you can to learn new skills and meet new people. Get your name out there...

But beyond all of that, focus on improving your physical, mental, and emotional health. Improve yourself and you'll continue to improve your career and your freelance career success.
*Is it worth it?*
I know you're asking that question. Is the life of a freelance editor worth the 10-hour work days (and only getting paid for eight or fewer) and potential frustrations that come from working from home? Is working as your own boss worth the uncertainty of income that is inevitable in this field? You'll have to answer those

questions for yourself, but I can answer that yes, it has been worth all of that for me.

I heard as much as you did that I was wasting my time majoring in religion. I let myself worry about my future income and productivity for more hours than I'd care to admit, but eventually I realized I wasn't going to get paid to worry any more than I get paid to write blogs for my website and post on social media. Instead of worrying about it, I could be writing books (like this one!), seeking out new, fantastic clients and getting to know new authors and editors. When I focused my energy into doing all of the work I love to do, I eventually discovered that *I was getting paid to read books*. What humanities major wouldn't be absolutely *thrilled* with that kind of life?

I love writing. I love reading. I love editing books in my niche. I get lost in the work. I work from home—a place I make my own and feel safe and comfortable in—or on the road, wherever that road takes me. I meet and read the ideas of fascinating people. I write about what I'm interested in and people read and are inspired by my words. I have the flexibility to travel and continue to work. I have the time to learn new technology and skills.

Thanks to my humanities degree, I have the ability to learn new software and editing techniques, the skills to do the work I love and do it well, and the attitude for success that drives me to keep moving forward in slow and big work months alike.

I love what I do, and I'm a big fan of my boss. ;)

This career—this editing life—isn't without its difficulties and setbacks, but as a humanities major, you are *primed* for this work.

Use your humanities major way of being to your advantage and show the publishing world—and anyone who questions your value in a money-driven world—**all the amazing things a humanities major can do**.

# Appendices

A. Resources for Freelancers
B. Niche Zone Worksheet
C. Freelancer's Day Planning Worksheets

# Appendix A. Resources for Freelancers

**For Your Editing Work:**
These helpful webpages are easy reference points on grammar, punctuation, proofreading and copyediting marks, word usage, etc.

*The Writing Mechanic's Favorite!* Grammar Girl:
> http://www.quickanddirtytips.com/grammar-girl

Merriam Webster Dictionary:
> https://www.merriam-webster.com/

Oxford Dictionary:
> https://en.oxforddictionaries.com/grammar-tips

*CMOS* Proofreading Symbols:
> http://www.chicagomanualofstyle.org/tools_proof.html

NY Book Editors Copyediting Marks:
> http://nybookeditors.com/2013/06/copyediting-marks/


**Freelance Writing:**
Barefoot Writer: http://www.thebarefootwriter.com/

AWAI: https://www.awai.com/


**Business Plan Template for Creatives:**
Wonderlass: http://www.wonderlass.com/blog/how-to-write-a-business-plan-for-creatives-a-free-template/

**Business Brand Workshops/Courses:**
Wonderlass: http://www.wonderlass.com/free-courses/
http://www.wonderlass.com/courses-1/

**Podcasts:**
The Goal Digger Podcast – Jenna Kutcher

RISE Podcast – Rachel Hollis

Entrepreneurs on Fire – John Lee Dumas

Build Your Tribe – Chalene Johnson and Brock Johnson

**The EFA Editing Rates Table**: https://www.the-efa.org/rates/

**Self-Improvement Books on Kathrin's Shelf** ("What I Read & Re-Read!"):

*Oola: Finding Balance in an Unbalanced World*

*The Miracle Morning*, by Hal Elrod

*Girl, Wash Your Face*, by Rachel Hollis

# Appendix B. Niche Zone Worksheet

**Fill in the blanks below to start thinking through your skills, talents, likes, and dislikes in your current or future editing business.**

Subjects I'm interested in:
- 
- 
- 
- 

Subjects I know something about but that don't really interest me:
- 
- 
- 
- 

The editing services I'm good at:
- 
- 
- 
- 

The types of editing I like to do:
- 
- 
- 
- 

The types of editing projects I get excited to do:
- 
- 
-

- 

The kinds of authors I would like to work with have these qualities:
- 
- 
- 
- 

I think my niche is: _____.

I plan to offer these services: _____
_____ _____ _____.

*P.S. You're a rock star. Don't ever forget it. ;)*

# Appendix C. Freelancer's Day Planning Worksheets

## Freelancer's Day Planning Worksheet

Day: _____    Date: ___/___/_____    Office Location: _____

### Lifestyle Tasks
(Journaling, Exercise, Meditation, Reading, etc.)

- [ ]
- [ ]
- [ ]
- [ ]
- [ ]
- [ ]

**Paid Tasks**
- [ ]
- [ ]
- [ ]

**Unpaid Tasks**
- [ ]
- [ ]
- [ ]

**Projects in the Works**
_____
_____

**Upcoming Projects**
_____
_____

**Business Tasks**
- [ ]
- [ ]

### Warm Market Contacts to Make
_____

**Daily Self Care**    **Daily Personal Development**    **Daily Exercise**
_____

### How I'm Making the World a Better Place Today
_____
_____

*I love what I do...and I'm a BIG FAN of my Boss. ;)*

# Freelancer's Day Planning Worksheet

Day: _____  Date: ___ /___ /_____  Office Location: _____

## Lifestyle Tasks
*(Journaling, Exercise, Meditation, Reading, etc.)*

☐
☐
☐
☐
☐

### Paid Tasks

☐
☐
☐

### Unpaid Tasks

☐
☐
☐

| Projects in the Works | Upcoming Projects | Business Tasks |
|---|---|---|
| _____ | _____ | ☐ |
| _____ | _____ | ☐ |

### Warm Market Contacts to Make

_____

_____

Daily Self Care    Daily Personal Development    Daily Exercise

_____

### How I'm Making the World a Better Place Today

_____

_____

*I love what I do...and I'm a BIG FAN of my Boss. ;)*

# Freelancer's Day Planning Worksheet

Day: _____ Date: ___ / ___ / _____ Office Location: _____

## Lifestyle Tasks
(Journaling, Exercise, Meditation, Reading, etc.)

☐
☐
☐
☐
☐
☐

### Paid Tasks
☐
☐
☐

### Unpaid Tasks
☐
☐
☐

### Projects in the Works
_____
_____

### Upcoming Projects
_____
_____

### Business Tasks
☐
☐

### Warm Market Contacts to Make
_____
_____

Daily Self Care     Daily Personal Development     Daily Exercise
_____
_____

### How I'm Making the World a Better Place Today
_____
_____
_____

*I love what I do...and I'm a BIG FAN of my Boss. ;)*

# Freelancer's Day Planning Worksheet

Day: _____    Date: ___ /___ /_____    Office Location: _____

## Lifestyle Tasks
(Journaling, Exercise, Meditation, Reading, etc.)

- [ ]
- [ ]
- [ ]
- [ ]
- [ ]

### Paid Tasks                                         Unpaid Tasks

- [ ]                                                  - [ ]
- [ ]                                                  - [ ]
- [ ]

### Projects in the Works    Upcoming Projects         Business Tasks

_____            - [ ]
_____            - [ ]

### Warm Market Contacts to Make

_____
_____

### Daily Self Care    Daily Personal Development    Daily Exercise

_____

### How I'm Making the World a Better Place Today

_____
_____

*I love what I do...and I'm a BIG FAN of my Boss. ;)*

# Freelancer's Day Planning Worksheet

Day: _____    Date: ___ / ___ / _____    Office Location: _____

### Lifestyle Tasks
(Journaling, Exercise, Meditation, Reading, etc.)

☐
☐
☐
☐
☐
☐

**Paid Tasks**                              **Unpaid Tasks**

☐                                           ☐
☐                                           ☐
☐                                           ☐

**Projects in the Works**    **Upcoming Projects**    **Business Tasks**

_____    _____    ☐
_____    _____    ☐

### Warm Market Contacts to Make

_____
_____

**Daily Self Care**    **Daily Personal Development**    **Daily Exercise**

_____
_____

### How I'm Making the World a Better Place Today

_____
_____
_____

*I love what I do...and I'm a BIG FAN of my Boss. :)*

# About the Author

**Kathrin Herr** is a graduate of Simpson College with a BA in Religion and of Duke Divinity School with her MA is Christian Studies.

In her almost eight years of freelance editing experience as The Writing Mechanic, she's learned a whole lot about what NOT to do to be successful...but as she works through the muck, she constantly recognizes how valuable her humanities degrees are to her career, her ability to learn and grow, and—maybe most importantly—to her growth and development as a person.

**They call our degrees "useless." But Kathrin knows, as you do, the power they have instilled in us.**

Kathrin is a Life Story Coach who has worked with self-published authors, established business professionals, academics, newbies, and veteran authors, all with the common goal of helping them share their knowledge and experience—their stories. She would love to hear your story and help you share it with the world.

**Find Kathrin Online:**
Website: www.KathrinHerr.com
Facebook: @kathrinmherr
Instagram: @kathrin_no_e
EFA Profile: https://bit.ly/2xNfhLx

# Acknowledgements

There are too many names to mention here, so I'll acknowledge you all in groups. I hope I have told you each personally how much having each of you in my life has changed me and helped me grow...and in that you should each recognize yourself here:

**To my family and friends** (these I will name): Michael, Mom, Dad, Jen, Jimi, Katie: You all rock. You've kept me sane in all my freelance craziness, and I couldn't do what I do without your support. Many of you read parts or the entirety of this book and made sure I wasn't talking crazy even when I was acting crazy. Love you all.

**To my students** who slogged through my teaching and soaked up everything you could from my messy career to start your own in editing: Thanks for sticking with me. I'm inspired by YOU even more than you were by me. Trust me on that.

**To my mentors**: Each of you pulled me forward in this editing life at one point or another. Thanks for pulling me along even when I was reluctant.

**To my clients**: Thank you for taking a leap of faith and working with me. You trusted me with your work, and I'm honored that I could be the one you call "My Editor."

**To my fellow humanities majors**: Thanks for picking this life. Whether you've picked a more traditional route or sought out something unique to devote your working life to, we have a common experience of being grads of

big-question-asking majors, and that's something we'
always share.

**To my readers**: This should be obvious, but I'm so grateful you picked up and took the time to read my book. I hope to see you all out here in the publishing world.

If there is ever anything I can do to help support you in this career—this life of potential freedom—let me know.

I mean that.

www.ingramcontent.com/pod-product-compliance
Lightning Source LLC
LaVergne TN
LVHW051519070426
835507LV00023B/3188